# Publishing from Your PhD

*For David*

# Publishing from Your PhD

*Negotiating a Crowded Jungle*

DR NICOLA F. JOHNSON

Routledge
Taylor & Francis Group
LONDON AND NEW YORK

First published 2011 by Gower Publishing

Published 2016 by Routledge
2 Park Square, Milton Park, Abingdon, Oxon OX14 4RN
711 Third Avenue, New York, NY 10017, USA

*Routledge is an imprint of the Taylor & Francis Group, an informa business*



**British Library Cataloguing in Publication Data**
Publishing from your PhD : negotiating a crowded jungle.
1. Dissertations, Academic--Publishing. 2. Scholarly publishing. 3. Scholarly periodicals. 4. Manuscripts--Editing. 5. Manuscript preparation (Authorship)
6. Universities and colleges--Graduate work.
I. Johnson, Nicola F., 1976-
808'.02-dc22

ISBN 9780566091629 (pbk)

**Library of Congress Cataloging-in-Publication Data**
Johnson, Nicola F., 1976-
Publishing from your PhD : negotiating a crowded jungle / by Nicola F. Johnson.
p. cm.
Includes bibliographical references and index.
ISBN 978-0-566-09162-9 (pbk.)
1. Scholarly publishing. 2. Doctor of philosophy degree. I. Title.
Z286.S37J64 2010
070.5--dc22

2010024660

# Contents

# List of Figures

# List of Tables

# Acknowledgements

I am grateful to the following people who made significant contributions to this monograph:

- Russell Walton for his quality proofreading and editing. I doubt I could recommend someone more highly.
- The academics who feature in this book. You are each an inspiration to me and I hope that, through this book, what you share will benefit countless others.
- Sean Maguire of Already Yesterday Photography for his terrific work and sincere friendship.
- Michelle Eady and Keira-Lee Metcalfe for their thorough feedback surrounding the journal profiling checklist.
- This book was made possible via a small research grant awarded by the Technology and Learning Research Group (TALR), from the Faculty of Education, a member in 2009 of the Information and Communication Technology Research Institute (ICTR) research strength, University of Wollongong, New South Wales, Australia.
- Thank you to Ashgate and Gower for their excellent publishing support.
- A final thank you goes to my parents Warwick and Suzanne for their continual support and faith in me, and to my husband David for his sparkle, his humour and his delight in the everyday.

# Introduction: Navigating a Jungle – No Worn Paths

So you have got your PhD. Perhaps you have submitted your thesis for examination and are thinking, 'Right, where shall I publish?' But now, you have a whole new jungle to navigate. Let me introduce you to this new environment.

Picture a jungle in your mind if you can. A jungle is always crowded. Tangles of vines, swarms of mosquitoes and the plethora of trees make creating a path a difficult process. Navigating a jungle proposes difficulties even for experienced trekkers. Inevitably, the drenching rain, uneven ground and the lack of landmarks make for an eventful journey. Yet, the imposition on your persona due to the lack of space and vistas make for slow progress.

The jungle is ruthless. It does not care whether you survive or not. The cruel or harsh world is cut-throat and invokes the need to play a survival game. Many fail. Many try only once or twice. Many do not reach their final destination, let alone a temporary one. A jungle is largely impenetrable unless you know what you are doing.

Navigating a jungle is akin to that of entering unmarked territory. The known paths or trajectories are not present. There is no well-trodden path to follow. There are many bugs, draining humidity, miserable rain, not to mention the exertion of blood, sweat and tears, as you seek to survive the journey from point A to point B. Yet, point B often changes. Point B has a tendency to move; indeed, it moves further away. At times, point A is no longer the starting point.

A jungle is uninviting. Much is unknown. Dangers lie hidden with unknown tracks, coarse undergrowth and relentless thick scrub. But if you were on a jungle safari (though you would undoubtedly have to sign a disclaimer), the dangers would be played down. The focus would be made on the end goal – the final destination – of which a simple trek would suffice. This trek would involve simple preparation, careful conduct, thoughtful navigation and assumed success, or, in other words – for one part of the jungle – condensing a section of your PhD thesis, checking for journal conventions, submitting it to a journal, and then waiting to receive confirmation of its acceptance.

But, being in a jungle is exhilarating. The challenge, the pressure and the desire to 'master' the environment is intense. But there is a price that must be paid in order to successfully navigate the jungle. There are many hurdles that take various forms – bugs, heat, exhaustion, hunger, thirst and the dark and cold of night. You need stamina (a thick skin) to survive the harsh world of academia. This book endeavours to shed light on the path you must take to navigate the mazes within academia. This is an untrodden path unique to every researcher – especially those who employ 'abstract' or 'critical' theoretical frameworks in their research – and each journey through the jungle is different. However, because there is little literature about this nascent expedition, this book seeks to illuminate the processes and difficulties of publishing in journals and culling your finely honed thesis into small chunks, which is a complex task to which few admit.

The metaphor of this crowded jungle provides analogous benefit when we apply it to the navigation of publishing from your PhD thesis. It is the author's experience that this crowded jungle is a frustrating complex system characterised by fierce competitiveness, where only the fittest survive. This chapter will outline the scope of the following chapters and delineate the realm of its focus.

Few academics (if any) talk about rejections. However, rejections of articles and book proposals are actually very frequent. Despite this, it seems that when someone admits they have received a rejection, it is deemed to be admitting failure and so it consequently does not exist – it is something kept quiet, relegated to a sobbing session in a storeroom. I aim to remove the secrecy and encourage us, as academics, to admit that publishing is a challenge and takes a confounded amount of time.

*Publishing from Your PhD* precisely focuses on providing nascent researchers with emotional and collegial support often not available in academia. It seeks to dispel nepotistic notions of superiority that place professors and such on a pedestal. The text specifically illuminates the difficulty in having written in the PhD thesis genre and rewriting it to suit the genre of journal articles, with the caveat that it does not deal with the 'how' of academic writing in general. What this book does do is give you the strategies and 'know-how' you need to successfully publish not only from your PhD thesis, but from your future research projects.

If searching the Internet, you will find websites expounding advice on how to format your PhD into a book. There is little that talks about how to take parts of your PhD and condense it into appropriate journal articles, that is, transferring a thesis of up to 100,000 words into smaller chunks of articles of 4,000, 6,000, 8,000 or 10,000 words. In Part Two of this book, I illustrate the ups and downs of established academics who are able to offer insight as to how they went about publishing from their PhD and during their careers. They give helpful advice that is of crucial need within academia worldwide.

## THE JUNGLE IS CROWDED

A jungle is dense with obstacles. This crowded nature is reflected in the competition for space, and the relentless imposition on others who seek to carve out a path. There is no easy path to take and no one is there ready to lead you by the hand. Navigating a path through a crowded jungle is an independent and arduous journey. But once you reach the final destination, the reward is worth the effort, and your confidence increases to subsequently navigate a new path in search of the next destination.



The process which you go through to have a doctorate conferred is complex and challenging. It is a significant achievement, if not the highest achievement in your life (to have a PhD bestowed). However, a PhD only teaches you the basics needed for beginning your academic career. It is not meant to win you a Nobel prize or other great honour. The PhD is the stepping stone needed to commence your research and academic career. Therefore, publishing from your doctorate is not the be-all and end-all. You have the rest of your career to publish, and the research conducted in your PhD provides you with the scaffold you need to publish in the future. However, you should publish from your doctorate due to it being a significant piece of work for you as an individual. Publishing is part of establishing your research profile and is especially crucial when going for tenure. If you hate your PhD or are disinterested in it, that is very sad. It should provide you with much that you can publish. It should give you impetus for where you can go next in your career, what you can build on for the future.

There is consistent pressure on early career academics to publish, publish, publish. But not unless they have been awarded their PhD – considered by most to be the starting step of an academic career. So while the pressure is on to obtain the title, and then obtain a permanent position, and then publish journal articles, there is little support available to researchers in the nascent stage of their careers.

When I submitted my hard-earned PhD, I started work on compiling articles for journals. I did not really know what I was doing but I thought I did. I learnt the hard way and found the process to be enlightening, though somewhat damaging to my ego. When I received the positive feedback on my thesis from my examiners, I was convinced that it deserved to be published. Therefore, why was I having such a hard time? This book clearly explicates the difficulties and challenges of the progression. One of the difficulties associated with this area, as I have personally found, is that while supervisors (advisors) are responsible for a student's candidature and thesis completion, they are not obligated to help you publish once a thesis has been submitted, passed and conferred. It remains that many early career academics are positioned in unmarked territory with no signposts, paths or directions.

Now that I have finished and been awarded my PhD, I still need to remember and reflect on the fact that I am an early career researcher. That means I am just starting out. I have completed five years of postgraduate study, which simply means that I am able to now *begin* my academic career. Though a PhD is a significant project that is demanding and all-encompassing, fulfilling the requirements only represents the completion of an apprenticeship. If you have a doctorate, you have demonstrated to the academic community that you have proven your cerebral worth, so therefore you need to claim your place within academia by publishing from your dissertation.[1]

It should be noted that had I read Abby Day's *How to Get Research Published in Journals* (1996), or even her second edition (2008), I would have been far better prepared. This book does not try to copy or replace Day's work, and I have found her text to be the most insightful and user-friendly to read during the literature review for this book. It is an easy read and it is tremendously pertinent about how you should write an article for a journal. This current book cannot beat it and does not try to; it is a complement to Day's text, and gives narratives of various academics and their struggles, while also candidly explaining my own struggles throughout the text. The book you are now reading is a candid exposé of the lives of academics that meets the need for a monograph with comprehensive discussion of the multiple issues, illustrated with real-life examples from a variety of fields.

There is an interesting nexus between expectations of publishing success and the necessity of this success, despite its lack of predictability. Not only

1 Thesis and dissertation are used interchangeably.

do expectations for successful publishing occur in order to attract higher degree by research students, obtain research grants and successfully achieve promotion, the weighting or quality of the journal significantly impacts these future prospects. However, what is not discussed is that, in reality, the wait is long and predictions of success are unreliable.

## NEW TO THE JUNGLE?

This section is for you if you have never published before. As one of my friends related the other day, she had written an assignment for her Masters degree research project. After submitting it, she was informed by the academic who marked her assignment that she should publish the results. For her, this was a frightening thought because this was a new jungle to navigate. Where to start? Like her, you may have obtained high grades in your assessments, but how do you go about writing an article for a journal? My advice to her is presented below.



The first thing is to identify in what field your work lies. Business management? Information systems? Does your work fit into educational fields such as early childhood? Educational leadership? Pedagogy? Computers in education? Then do a web or library search for journals that have that field referred to in their title. The second thing to do is ascertain the approximate word length that each of those journals require. Next, have a look at the word length of your assignment and decide which journal might be best. After that you need to search for more journals that have a similar word-length expectation and have published research similar to the type of research you conducted. Obtain at least three different journal titles. Finally, you then need to read the rest of this book.

## CLARIFYING THE JUNGLE: AN OVERVIEW OF EACH CHAPTER

Chapter 1 – Supplies are Needed, Packing the Backpack: What Others have Written – summarises the previously written literature surrounding the act of publishing. It delineates what this book is and what it is not. Chapter 2 – Hacking a Path Through Unknown Territory – is a personal narrative and explains my navigation of the many paths throughout my academic jungle and shares the mishaps and accidents of the journey. Chapter 3 – Navigating New Terrain: The Demise of the Book? – discusses whether the book as a genre is in a state of demise, and considers what our attitude towards electronic books should be. It examines contemporary issues such as digitisation, open access, authority and legitimacy of knowledge, and publishing your thesis as a book. It debates the merits and weighting of books and other genres, including journal articles. In Chapter 4 – Flies, Gnats and Wasps: Negotiating the Gatekeepers – I give authentic rejection rate examples from a range of peer-reviewed journals in order to demonstrate the fact that we as academics are all competing for what is a low acceptance rate. Various paradigmatic, methodological and ideological positions are brought to light in Chapter 5 – The Night is Black: No Black or White in Academia – which demonstrates the many shades of grey evident in academia. Probably the most important chapter of this book is Chapter 6 – Stamina is Needed for Survival: Choosing the Right Journal – which will convince you of the necessity to carefully choose the right journal and gives explicit detail about how to profile a journal to ensure it is the right 'fit' for your work. Dealing with rejection and criticism (constructive or not) is the topic of Chapter 7 – Fighting the Heat, Hunger and Thirst: Dealing with Rejection. Chapter 8 – Thorny Bushes and Muddy Swamps: Things That Slow You Down – discusses the obstacles that can be avoided when navigating the jungle of academia. Chapter 9 – The Final Destination Has Moved, Hack Another Path: The Process of Culling and Prioritising – thrashes out the various aspects that must be considered when changing your thesis from its original audience to that of a particular journal's, and then carving up your thesis into appropriate article-sized chunks.

Chapters 10–15 share verbatim interviews with established academics, profiling their careers, and offering pertinent advice for those who seek to carve out a path through the jungle. Though each of the academics featured in this book reside in Australia, the experiences shared have a broad, international focus. In Chapter 10, Professor Jan Herrington relates how she published from her PhD, and explains the drama of the quintessential paper. Professor Paul Chandler relates the controversy of an article he wrote from his PhD in Chapter 11. In Chapter 12, Professor Lori Lockyer explains the benefits of collaboration and joint authorship. Professor Jan Wright discusses the difficulties of publishing during your PhD in Chapter 13. She also talks about the phenomena of publishing your thesis as a book. In Chapter 14, Professor Wilma Vialle discusses the importance of audience when crafting publications, and highlights the limitations of being placed within a 'small' field. In Chapter 15, Professor Sara Dolnicar explicates the ethics surrounding her turbo road to success.

The conclusion – Negotiating the Crowded Jungle: Acknowledge Successful Navigation – coalesces the discussion of this book, and leaves you better prepared for navigating unmarked territory. Come with me and learn about the challenges, pitfalls and successes of negotiating a crowded jungle.

# 1 Supplies are Needed, Packing the Backpack: What Others have Written

## ARMING THE PACK FOR THE DESTINATION AHEAD

This chapter summarises the previously written 'help' books and explains what others have written about negotiating the beginning scholar's pathway. Though these books are valuable, they do not explain the frustration and real-life stories, and the 'how-to' of publishing from your PhD. There is a lot of literature of 'how' to put a thesis together, which nicely fit alongside your advisor's or supervisor's role in helping you to construct your thesis.

In reviewing the literature for this book, I found a number of helpful publications that discuss the 'how' of writing, so it is important that this text does not replicate these previously published works, nor does it try to. The following books proved to be very helpful to me, yet they are dissimilar to this book in that this monograph a) focuses on my particular experiences as an early career researcher, or beginner academic, b) provides a contemporary perspective on the plights of publishing, and c) shares the trajectories of established academics. In 2010, the following books are dated and perhaps have not focused on the competitive nature and continuing struggle of publishing, whilst some also exclude the present-day nature of electronic publishing. However, you may find these books in your university library, and each can be helpful, especially as they have been written by experienced academics.

*Publishing in Refereed Academic Journals: A Pocket Guide* (Kenway, Gough and Hughes 1998, Deakin Centre for Education and Change). This helpful book is very short and small in size (76 pages, 15 cm x 12 cm). Much of the instructive book is written in bullet points for a quick read. It does not discuss issues in depth, and is not focused on publishing from your PhD from the perspective of an early career researcher. It focuses on how to write articles for specific journals, which is of interest to any academic, but the authors admit it is not comprehensive.

*How to Survive Peer Review* (Wager, Godlee and Jefferson 2002, BMJ Books). This useful book is also very short (62 pages), but is mainly written from a medical science perspective for healthcare professionals. It defines peer review and discusses how to be a reviewer, both formally and informally, but it only lightly covers the topic of dealing with rejection (which is what its title insinuates). *Publishing from Your PhD* dedicates a whole chapter (Chapter 7) to the traumatic experience of dealing with rejection.

*Writing for Academic Success: A Postgraduate Guide* (Craswell 2005, Sage). While this text focuses on how to write a thesis, its ninth and final chapter discusses 'Journal Article and Book Publication' (16 pages). While this chapter offers specific and useful advice, it does not address the issues of how to craft 4,000–9,000-word articles from a thesis consisting of approximately 90,000+ words. It does, however, discuss the pros and cons of publishing while still in student candidature.

All of these preceding books give dot point directions to researchers and give brief overviews about academic writing. A comprehensive series of books has been written by Rebecca Boden, Jane Kenway and Debbie Epstein entitled the 'Academic's Support Kit'.[1] The six-volume 'kit' covers, in order, *Building your Academic Career; Getting Started on Research; Writing for Publication; Teaching and Supervision; Winning and Managing Research Funding*; and *Building Networks.* Volume 3 *Writing for Publication* devotes one chapter (24 pages) to 'Publishing Articles in Academic Journals'. These books are delightfully delivered with humour and practical points, and share anonymous anecdotes about various intricacies of academia.

A 2010 publication by Aitchison, Kamler and Lee (Routledge) also focuses on publishing from your doctorate. Entitled, *Publishing Pedagogies for the Doctorate and Beyond*, it details some difficulties about publishing while being a student and also highlights how to negotiate conflicting reviews while working on a resubmission. It also argues the need for doctoral students to be supported in their efforts to publish, while also detailing how doctoral students might be mentored, and encouraged to network within multidisciplinary research writing groups. The edited volume is distinct from this work as it focuses on 'socially situated theories of pedagogical practice' (2010: 6). It offers many ideas concerning how to go about publishing from your PhD, and in that

1 Although Boden, Kenway and Epstein (2005, Sage) authored the Academics Support Kit as a whole, no two of the volumes feature the authors in the same order. A classic case of sharing credit around a group, as well as being proof that co-authoring can work.

sense, is similar to this book, as it seeks to develop knowledge, skill and confidence in order to publish successfully in scholarly avenues. Aitchison et al.'s edited collection is a complementary text to this one as its focus is on the infrastructure evident in universities and how the scholarly publication of doctoral research might be best 'facilitated, managed or taught' (2010: 2).

## PREVIOUS NAVIGATION

Many of the 'how-to' books cover a range of writing, not just for journals, but include information on the practicalities of writing books, research grants, conference papers and speeches. Other publications detail how to work with publishers, and negotiate contracts (Cantor 1993, Greenwood Press; Luey 2002, Cambridge University Press), which provide valuable information. In terms of the 'how' to go about writing, I recommend Abby Day's *How to Get Research Published in Journals* (1996, Gower) or her later edition (2008, Gower), as well as Black et al.'s (1998, Kogan Page) *500 Tips for Getting Published: A Guide for Educators, Researchers and Professionals*. These books provide fundamental advice about how to construct text and recommend good writing habits from which academic authors can benefit. I wish I had read those two books before I started submitting sole-authored articles for publication (based on my PhD).



Cantor's *A Guide to Academic Writing* (1993, Greenwood Press) is a matter-of-fact book about academic writing, and makes a valuable contribution of things to keep in mind when assessing the final version of your article that you wish to submit for review. 'Be original and present only new information and fresh insights' (Cantor 1993: 13). It seems obvious, but as I will allude to, sometimes it is hard to see the wood for the trees in the jungle, therefore, asking yourself whether what you have to present is actually 'fresh' is a worthwhile question. Another obvious point Cantor makes, is that while many people will read the title, not many will read the article. Therefore, a clear, informative and catchy title is important. Black et al. (1998) state you should make the title self-explanatory and interesting. Whet the reader's appetite for more!

Beth Luey's fourth edition of the *Handbook for Academic Authors* (2002, Cambridge University Press) covers a wide range of writing. Luey devotes 11 pages to the process and dilemma of whether to turn your thesis into a book. She discusses the 'thesis-book continuum' (2002: 40–41), whether you need a complete overhaul of your thesis to write a book, or whether limited, cosmetic revision is needed. If you are considering publishing your thesis in the book genre, this book may prove to be very helpful to you.

The most detailed book I have read is Anne Sigismund Huff's *Writing for Scholarly Publication* (1999, Sage), which is explicit in focus and comprehensive in nature. It includes thorough checklists that you can use to review the quality of your own article or a peer's. These checklists include the introduction and rationale of an article, whether you use quantitative or qualitative methodology, theory development or case studies. This text and Day's monograph give very direct advice concerning going from nothing on paper to the steps needed to take to submit an article. Again, *Publishing from Your PhD* does not attempt to provide this facility.

So why would you read this book rather than the ones mentioned above? Those books are in dot point form or are general, for example, they cover the whole range of writing in the academic realm (grants, books, articles, cover letters, résumés). Aitchison et al.'s (2010) work concentrates on how to teach doctoral students to write, publish and edit. This book focuses on explaining the real-life stories of successful academics, and putting a name and face to the lived experiences of these people. It creates an insight into academia and conveys a sense of emotional support that is not readily available when competing in the crowded jungle of academia. In the writing of this book, the monographs cited above have influenced me, but this book is not meant to replicate or replace these. If you have no idea how to draft an article, read those books. If you do not know how to turn your article from a good one into a great one, read one of those books. If you want to obtain an understanding of the nuances and intricacies of publishing the findings of your PhD and negotiating the crowded jungle of academic performance, then this is the book for you.



## GOOD FORM AND CONTENT

Based on these books (and from consultation with some of the featured academics in this book) I have developed three checklists that detail how to ensure that your article is ready for journal submission. The first is a checklist to make sure your article is refined enough in form to warrant submitting, the second about the content of the article, and the third, the checklist for ensuring your abstract is of high quality. The following checklists summarise the literature published in this field and give advice on form and content of your article. These should be considered and checked off before you submit an article to a journal (or conference) for review. The two checklists featured below (Table 1.1 and Table 1.2) focus on form and content (Epstein, Kenway and Boden 2005; Kenway, Gough and Hughes 1998).

**Table 1.1 Form checklist**

| | N/A | Check |
|---|---|---|
| Length of article | | |
| Abbreviations | | |
| References | | |
| Spacing | | |
| Margins | | |
| Acronyms (remove or use sparingly) | | |
| Explanation of jargon (or remove) | | |
| Spelling (UK, US, AUS) | | |
| Headings | | |
| Subheadings | | |
| Tables | | |
| Figures | | |
| Footnotes | | |
| Abstract (length and style) | | |
| Author affiliation | | |
| Cover letter | | |
| Title page | | |
| Punctuation | | |
| Author details (names and contact details) | | |
| Word count | | |
| Conflicts of interest | | |
| Ethics | | |
| Acknowledgements (reviewers, funding source, collaborators, research assistants) | | |
| Keywords | | |
| Blinded (in-text and references list) | | |
| Short title (running head) | | |
| Font and size of text | | |
| Correct email address or online manuscript system account | | |
| Inclusion of nominated reviewers | | |
| Use of personal pronouns | | |
| Verb tense | | |
| Active or passive voice | | |
| Other | | |
| In summary – does your article conform to the style of the journal? | | |

*Source*: Influenced by Day (1996); Epstein, Kenway and Boden (2005); Kenway, Gough and Hughes (1998); Wager, Godlee and Jefferson (2002); Black et al. (1998); and Craswell (2005).

## Table 1.2 Content checklist

| **Is your article ...** | **Check** |
|---|---|
| well sequenced and organised? Does it have a logical flow? | |
| analytically adequate? | |
| theoretically adequate? | |
| stylistically adequate? | |
| methodologically adequate? | |
| a good read? | |
| original (not published elsewhere)? | |
| | |
| **Does your ...** | |
| title reflect the content of the article? | |
| article matter? | |
| introduction orient the reader? | |
| rationale justify the article? | |
| literature review succinctly summarise the literature? | |
| purpose feature on the first page? | |
| introduction state the contribution the article is making? | |
| article have appeal to the readership? | |
| article adequately interpret the findings? | |
| article justify the findings and why they matter and for whom? | |
| article include implications and applications of your findings? | |
| article describe areas for future research? | |
| conclusion restate and reinforce what you have said? | |
| article reference previously published articles from that journal? | |
| article present new information? | |
| | |
| **Do you ...** | |
| authorise the content and put your own stamp on it? | |
| initially obtain readers' attention? | |
| continue readers' interest in the article? | |
| state the limitations of the research? (May not be applicable to your field) | |
| bring new or fresh insights? | |
| introduce new data? | |
| use appropriate voice? (formal, informal, journalistic, etc) | |
| legitimate the conclusions you've made based on the methods you've employed in the research and the evidence you have provided? | |

*Source*: Influenced by Day (1996); Epstein, Kenway and Boden (2005); Kenway, Gough and Hughes (1998), Wager, Godlee and Jefferson (2002); Cantor (1993); and Craswell (2005).

There is a reason these checklists are long. The length of these checklists demonstrates the complexity associated with ensuring your article is a) worthy of submission, and b) worthy of publication. These checklists reflect the depth of explanation exhibited in the other texts I have mentioned as the checklists detail *how* to write within and for this genre. If you do not pay careful attention to the form and content of your article, you increase your chances of rejection, that is, the journal will not accept your article for publication, nor will they be interested in a revised submission. Day (2008) pointed out the high frustration levels of editors and reviewers when authors have been sloppy in attending to the conventions of the journal. It is important to write for the reader and have that specific reader in mind when you write your text. Readers are busy people. They need to quickly ascertain whether the article is relevant and useful to them (Day 1996). In fact, you should not suppose the reader knows what you are saying and why it is important. You must make that clear for them.



It should be noted right here, that one of the most important secrets of publishing success (in my opinion) is to ensure that you have not only chosen the right journal to which to submit your work, but that you have carefully tailored your article to the stylistic and ideological conventions of the journal. This is systematically discussed further in Chapter 6.

As these checklists have profiled what you should do, Kenway, Gough and Hughes (1998) poignantly and directly list what you should not do.

- don't show off;
- don't 'over-write';
- don't over-cite and over-quote others' work;
- don't plagiarise;
- don't develop so many themes in the paper that it loses its focus;
- don't slavishly follow the latest orthodoxy;
- don't use the journal as a final editing service;
- don't wait until you are completely satisfied with your paper;
- don't get defensive about criticism (Kenway, Gough and Hughes 1998: 42–3).

We will address how to take criticism in Chapter 7, and address the common fear of writing down your ideas and publishing your research. Chapter 4 will help to put things into perspective, as it relates the stark reality of high rejection rates, highlighting the small acceptance rates for which we, all of us – beginners and experienced academics alike – are competing. Each one of the points above deserves an anecdote as they are so important, and this book attempts to tell some of these stories. While they may be embarrassing in one context, if shared, they will prove supportive and helpful to the academic community.

Before inserting these checklists into this book, I asked some of the people I had interviewed their opinion on the credibility of them. I have used them as I have gone about constructing articles for journals, but I also wish that I had them available to me when I had just submitted my PhD dissertation for examination, and was ready to start publishing from my PhD.

The final checklist I include in this chapter is one for your abstract. Some academics like to write the abstract first before they write an article or conference. Others prefer to write the article or paper first, and then write the abstract. Whatever option suits you, it remains that the abstract is of crucial importance. If you are lucky enough for someone to read your title, then the next thing they will read (if they are interested) is your abstract. Only then might they read your article. As there is often a 'call for abstracts' for book chapters and conferences long before the paper or chapter is due, I thought it prudent to include the following checklist (Table 1.3). These criteria must be addressed when writing an abstract.

**Table 1.3 Abstract checklist**

| | **Check** |
|---|---|
| Word length | |
| Rationale for the research (why?) | |
| Methodology of the research (how?) | |
| Findings (what?) | |
| Implications and applications (if applicable) | |

*Source*: Influenced by Kenway, Gough and Hughes (1998).

## WHY NAVIGATE THIS PATH?

Why publish? Why publish in journals? There are many reasons to publish, but you must own these reasons. Day (2008) and Black et al. (1998) detail some reasons such as 'being famous' and 'making money', and while these are not really applicable in academia, it remains that in order to obtain tenure or promotion, you must publish. The old adage 'publish or perish' is a common mantra amongst academics.

Journal articles seem to be the be-all and end-all. Books may receive more points when counted in research assessment exercises, but journal articles seem to have more kudos, especially if the journal has a high impact factor (IF). Certain fields value books more than journal articles, others are vice versa. Journal articles tend to be valued more than other publications, but Kenway, Gough and Hughes (1998) argued that, in the field of humanities and social sciences, scholarly monographs are the most prestigious form of publication.

But why should we write? Huff (1999) aptly answers this question:

> *To share your ideas and fully participate in the scholarship of your field, you therefore must write. This is the first reason to pay attention to writing. Writing is not just a way of communicating conclusions from your scholarly endeavours, it is a more basic means of participating in scholarship itself. Our efforts to communicate, especially within the disciplining confines of the written word, help us develop an intrinsic understanding of the tacit norms and subtle nuances that characterize good scholarship. (Huff 1999: 5)*



Writing for publication is not only important. Writing down ideas and conceptual thinking is important for an academic's identity, for their development and for their thinking. In writing, my thoughts are actualised as I explore my world and argue for the place I have in it and for what I believe to be true. Writing captures moments in time and seals them there permanently. Like a diary, it reminds us of what we once were as it and we await new development. In addition, when we write something that is published, be it a diary entry, blog posting or journal article, it takes us back specifically to what we thought or were working on at the time, and often provokes a thought such as, 'Did I write that?', 'I forgot I wrote that', 'I can see why that did not get published', and pleasantly, 'Oh, that was quite good!'

There is always an idea, and/or a draft waiting to be crafted. But the text of writing provides security as it congeals scrambled thoughts and actualises possibilities. It invokes a sense of worth as print on paper implies accuracy and purpose. For me, writing is a way to learn and it also confirms what I have learned. It makes sense of the myriad of thoughts that cross my mind, as I carefully explain in 'black and white' what I mean (or what I think I mean at the time).

While the spoken word constructs learning, the written word is learning in actuality. As an educator, I seem to be very aware of when I am learning and through what forum, exemplified by:

When I think I learn.

When I write I learn.

When I do I learn.

When I create I learn.

When I talk I learn.

When I network I learn.



The sense of the real is confirmed in the written word just as the transcription of speech erases some ambiguity. Tone, inflection, colour and mood create vagueness or uncertainty in the spoken word but the written word does away with these temporary meanings to rely solely on the 'black and white', even though subjectivity can never be entirely expelled. That said, there is no black and white in academia. The subjectivity of academia dominates the jungle's landscape, making it hard to see paths, signposts or landmarks.

The importance of writing and its nexus with thinking is captured well with Huff's three questions:

> *How can I know what I think until I see what I write?*
> *How can I improve what I write until I clarify what I think?*
> *Think before you write. Then, write to help you rethink.*
>
> (Huff 1999: 7–8)

So, as academics, we need to write. We must write. But if it remains that we must publish, we must realise that we will never ever achieve the perfect manuscript that everyone loves and is so carefully and thoroughly explained that no one can or will argue with it. With the fallible nature of human beings, we should always be ready to admit our limitations, especially that of our research. Abby Day (2008) has said there are two types of articles – the ones that are perfect and never get published, and the others that are good enough and do. There is no use trying to craft an immaculate manuscript because it may be something you never, ever finish.

# 2 Hacking a Path Through Unknown Territory

Anyone who knows me knows that I am a terrible liar. My dreams of being an actor were quashed long ago when struggling to keep a straight face while telling my mother a white lie. I like candour. I find it refreshing. To me, there seems to be a lack of frankness in academia. Honesty is the best policy and I applaud sincerity and transparency. This is partly why I wrote this book. I believe that others can benefit from honesty; they can learn from our (and my) experiences. I seek to shed light on the intricacies, fallacies and perceived nepotism and gatekeeping of academia. There is quite a lot to learn about playing the academic game. The so-called unwritten rules are prevalent and have confounding consequences if they are not observed.

## LOOKING BACK

Publishing from my PhD was like hesitantly making my way through an uninviting, coarse jungle. I knew the rules and the objectives, but it was difficult as I tried to find a way through the thick, unforgiving scrub by myself. There was no lighted path. And when I spent days and hours hacking a particular path, months later I found it was the wrong way. So then I tried multiple paths concurrently and yet the trails were still unknown. I was too shy to ask for help, especially as I was aware that other academics were so busy with their own lives. When I did ask for help, the assistance only helped me walk a few more steps (which is better than nothing of course!). It did not result in reaching the final destination. That was because the persons whom I asked for help were not on the same path as me nor did they have the same objective; they did not help me navigate the thorns, the backlash of the branches and the density of the bush. It was up to me to make my own way. Every failed path was an affront to my mind – a knock to my confidence casting doubt on my ability to ever get through the jungle.

This chapter details the chronological journey of hacking a path through unknown territory. I did succeed, but it was not a perfect, easy path. I got through, but two paths were blocked. Three other paths were tested and navigated but took a terribly long time. My struggle is documented in the following text. Let me take you back to the time of my peak frustrations and share them with you.

## THERE IS NO WAY THROUGH

I am frustrated. It is September 19 2008 and I have published little. My frustration and struggle lies with my lack of success in being able to successfully publish the results of my PhD via the medium of refereed journal articles.

My PhD was entitled, 'Teenage Technological Experts: Bourdieu and the Performance of Expertise' which I submitted for examination in June (2007). Most people I have spoken to have had a somewhat similar reaction to my title and said, 'Oh, that sounds interesting.' I also think the topic is interesting. My thesis examiners were very pleased with what I produced. Some of the comments were:



> *'I commend and congratulate Ms Johnson for having produced a coherent, rigorous and thoughtful analysis of the intersection of a highly relevant contemporary issue'; the thesis 'makes a valuable contribution to the body of scholarship on young people and digital technologies'; and the thesis was 'an effective and original work of scholarship'.*

So, why did I have so much trouble publishing the results of my PhD? I have asked myself that very question countless times (as well as whether the question was accurate, and whether my experience was 'normal').

Let me explain the process I have been through. After submitting my thesis, I started to pull sections from my thesis together and split it up into what I thought were four coherent journal articles. I made sure I attended to stylistic conventions and instructions for authors, and submitted three journal articles based on my PhD to two A-star journals and one B journal (as of the 2008 Excellence in Research Australia (ERA) rankings, see Chapter 6). All three asked for substantial revisions and I resubmitted them early in 2008. I submitted a fourth article to an American journal but it was not sent out for review because the editor nicely explained that it was beyond their scope. I decided not to resubmit this article to an alternative journal as it consequently became one of my strongest chapters in my first book, *The Multiplicities of Internet Addiction* (Johnson 2009a).

Please note: these journals and articles are not being mentioned to discredit the journals, or dissuade you from submission. These journals, their editors, their editorial boards and their reviewers did me a favour. They were doing their job. I do recommend them as avenues for publication. Rather, this text represents the lived experience of what can happen with reviews, and the very real nature of rejections. Much of my struggle has been a result of my own ignorant fault. I am not criticising these journals. The timeline of my journey is presented in Figure 2.1.

## Article 1: 'Cyber-relations in the Field of Home Computer use for Leisure: Bourdieu and Teenage Technological Expertise' (Johnson 2009b)

I submitted Article 1 to the *British Journal of Sociology of Education* (BJSE) on 22/10/07. I was thrilled when BJSE asked for a resubmission on 5/2/2008. I submitted the revision on 24/4/2008. This revision was rejected on 16/8/2008. BJSE do not send papers out for a third review once they have been resubmitted. I received this email early on a Saturday morning, and subsequently spent the entire day revising the article. I submitted it that evening to the *Journal of Computer Mediated Communication* (JCMC) (c. 17/8/2008). Mistake number 803. I heard back from JCMC on the 18/9/2008 with another rejection. I consequently revised the article once more (and took a lot more time) and submitted it to *E-Learning* on 20/10/08. This was done with direct and explicit help from my academic supervisor. She made comments to me that confirmed my belief that I could not see the wood for the trees. Many of the suggestions she made were actually very obvious, and were part of my current knowledge about how to write articles. I just had not done those things. (Hence, why I have designed the checklists on 'form' and 'content' in Chapter 1.) This resulted in an acceptance from *E-Learning* on 6/3/2009, which stated eight minor points to address. I sent the revision to the editor via email stating how I had addressed each of the points within the accompanying attachment. The editor accepted the revision by promptly asking for my biographical note and that was that. This article was published in the second issue of the 2009 volume.

## Article 2: 'Teenage Technological Experts' Views of Schooling' (Johnson 2009c)

After submitting my article on 10/9/2007, *Australian Educational Researcher* asked me to resubmit with revisions on 23/5/2008 (eight months later). During this time, one of the reviewers was unable to complete the review due to illness, so the process was delayed. I submitted the revision on 8/8/2008. This resubmission was accepted on 16/10/2008. The article was published in the first issue of the 2009 volume.

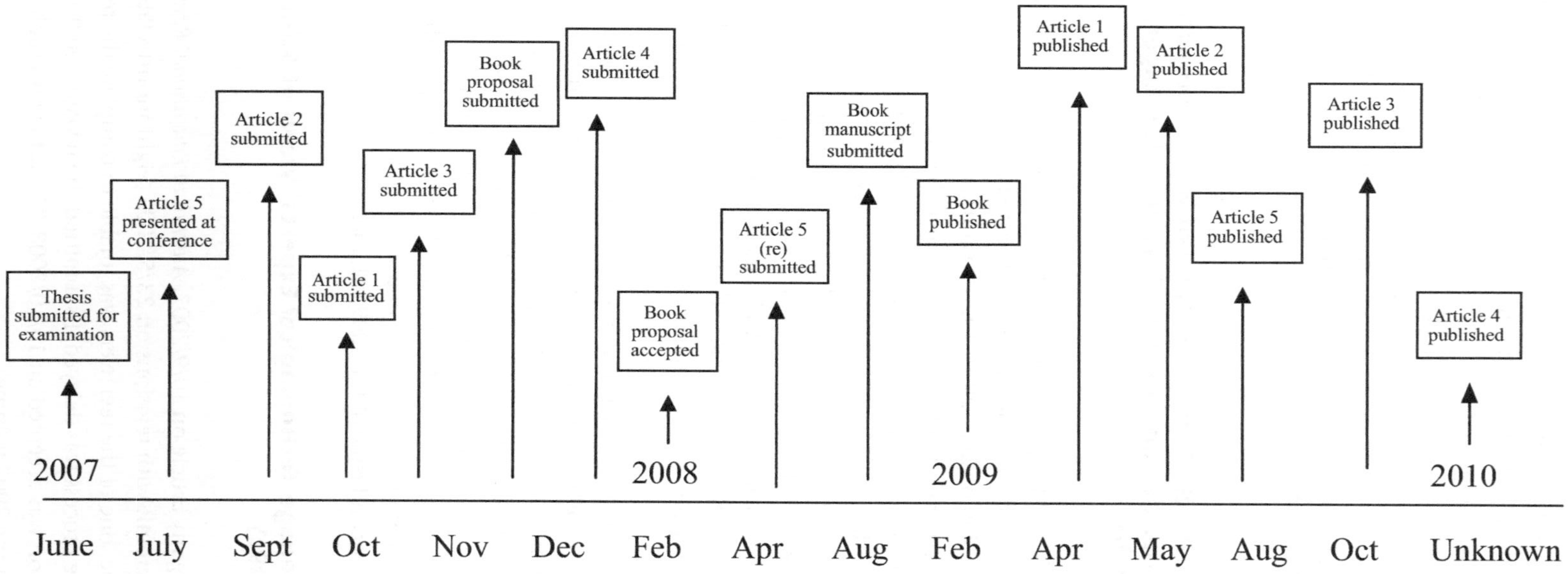


**Figure 2.1 Timeline (busily negotiating the jungle)**

## Article 3: 'Generational Differences in Beliefs about Technological Expertise' (Johnson 2009d)

I first submitted this article to the journal *New Zealand Journal Educational Studies* (NZJES) on 19/10/2007. NZJES asked me to resubmit on 22/3/2008. I submitted the revision on 17/4/2008. However, they did not receive the submission (failed email technology). Once I followed up, they explained the situation. In May, one of the co-editors emailed me stating that the article was being processed. In December 2008, I was informed (after a carefully couched query about the table of contents) that it was accepted. When I asked for a PDF copy of the publication to verify its publication, I was informed that the article had been held over to the next year due to a lack of space in the 2008 volume. I was required to do further editing in March 2009. I made the corrections within a week, and the article was published online around August 2009.

## Article 4: 'Contesting Binaries: Teenage Girls as Technological Experts' (Johnson, 2009f)



I submitted the article (the title also changed during the revisions) to *Gender and Education* (c. December 2007), which was rejected outright after review. Based on these reviews, I revised the article and resubmitted it to *Gender, Technology and Development* (GTD) on 10/9/08. It took a fair amount of time to decide where to resubmit the article (after I made the suggested corrections) as *Gender and Education* is not only the top journal in its field, but is arguably one of the few that discusses issues of gender in education. It has a high impact factor (IF) but, as of 14/12/09, GTD did not have a recorded IF (but in one ERA category, it is ranked 'A' and in another it is ranked 'B'). However, given the circumstances – that of being an early career researcher, and that there were few similar journals – I was happy to simply receive an acceptance. I emailed the managing editor on 25/2/09 to enquire about the status of my manuscript, but received the disappointing response that stated they had not received my manuscript on the 10/9/08. It seems that my email had not 'gone through'. There went another five wasted months. This mistake was blamed on technology! Lesson number 867, make sure you receive a receipt for your submitted article! GTD gave me feedback from three reviewers on 10/10/09. I sent a revision in after three weeks. The editor then gave me further feedback and I submitted an additional revision one week later. It was accepted for publication on 3/12/09.

## Article 5: 'Exchanging Online Narratives for Leisure: A Legitimate Learning Space' (Johnson 2009e)

On 7/10/08, I submitted an article of a theoretical nature with a small data set (not based on my PhD) to the *International Journal of Emerging Technologies and Society* (IJETS). It was confirmed on 21/10/08 that it would be sent out for review. This article was previously submitted and rejected by *Learning, Media and Technology* (who refused to send it out for review), and then once I revised it again, was rejected by the *Journal of Computer Mediated Communication* after two reviewers recommended it be refused. However, an earlier version of this same paper was accepted, refereed and presented at a conference in 2007. An associate professor and a senior lecturer also commented on this article before I initially submitted it for journal review. After further review and more editing, this article was published in the first issue of the 2009 volume of IJETS which, to me, demonstrated that not only did the article need a lot of work, but that I had contributed to my own failure because I submitted the article to unsympathetic avenues for publication.

### Article 6: 'Using an Instructional Design Model to Evaluate a Blended Learning Subject in a Pre-service Teacher Education Program'



An article I wrote about teaching in higher education (not my PhD) was submitted to an A-star journal on 10/2/09. I received extensive reviewers' comments on 17/8/09, which were somewhat discrepant. I responded to these as best I could, and worked towards addressing the concerns of the reviewer whose 'take' I most agreed with. I resubmitted the article on 9/10/09, but along with some more detailed feedback, the article was rejected on 7/12/09. The article needed more work, more focus and an alternative avenue for publication. It was not the right 'fit'. These examples demonstrate the length of time it takes to not only get feedback, but also to have your work accepted for publication.

## THE STONE WALL

In 2006, I was contacted by a professor who had a contract to edit a new book and wanted to know if I would like to contribute a chapter. I immediately said 'yes' and was both flattered and thrilled by the opportunity. I worked very hard over the year to complete what I thought fitted the guidelines that he had shared. A couple of months before the copy was due, I sent the draft (still a work in progress) to the editor requesting his comment, to ensure I was on the right track. He did not reply. About two months after the copy was due – of course I met the deadline, while the others were late and so, again, he put off reading my chapter – I received an email with a hugely damning review attached to it along with the editor's concerns about the manuscript. I was then advised that my chapter was no longer required as I had failed to write to the requirements, indeed, I had missed the mark completely.

The content and the focus of that book is unnecessary to include (as is the editor's name), however, this was an example of where I, as an early career academic who had not yet had her doctorate conferred, was unsupported. The whole effort was lost and I subsided into a miry swamp of self-loathing for many days. I really questioned my intellect, competence and ability to write. This path hit a dead end in the form of a stone wall.

## FACING REALITY?

The rejections of Article 1, Article 4, Article 5 and the book chapter put me in a spin. I was extremely disheartened after the first rejection and about ready to slit my wrists after the second. A more pragmatic mindset rose to the surface and I thought to myself, 'I must be doing something (or a lot of things) wrong.' There was an obvious need to do something different. I asked my employment supervisor to read and give me feedback about Article 1. What she said was not only helpful, but practical and realistic. We discussed what journal it should be submitted to. The difficulty of publishing from your completed PhD is more difficult than having the results of a research project and then determining which journal to write for. To me, that is an ideal situation. Having a target audience and readership in mind before you write and submit the article is idyllic. When you have a thesis that is (only) written for two examiners, it is not only difficult to carve it up into small chunks for suitable publication, it is difficult to go back to scratch and start constructing an article for a journal's audience (and editorial board).



### You Can't Give What You Don't Have

It seemed the reviewers of Article 1 wanted data I did not have and a higher level of theoretical engagement than what I did in my PhD. The reviewers of Article 5 were methodologically opposed to the theoretical nature of the article. The reviewers of Article 4 did not regard my work as being theoretical enough. So what did I do? I tried to carve another path and I submitted these articles to other or less prestigious journals. I changed or lowered my expectations but still worked towards the same objective – quality publications in quality journals. Within the jungle, though the night is black, the expedition is not black and white. The grey of academia will be expounded further in Chapter 5.

## GETTING NOWHERE FAST

My husband suggested I was aiming for journals that were too prestigious, especially given the fact that my PhD was a small study (which alludes to his philosophical perspective). I acknowledge there are many other variables, including a notable one that the small-scale success I have had with writing a thesis and research grants does not transpose to the genre of journal articles. But these rejections caused me to think that perhaps my PhD was not deemed 'good' beyond the three examiners (two professors and one associate professor) who read and assessed my thesis. It caused me to think that perhaps I was not good at writing. It made me think that I had chosen the wrong career. It seemed to me that I might be better at stacking shelves or picking fruit instead of pretending to be an academic.

It is obvious that these lines of thought were/are an indication of poor mental health and that I was well advised to take up more realistic thoughts that were more appropriate. Reviewers' revisions are generally very helpful. This all leads to further improvement in writing, argument, analysis and future publications. Rejections indicate that your homework has not been done. Prior research about a journal is absolutely crucial (see Chapter 6). Dealing with rejection is a common experience that can be rationally dealt with (see Chapter 7).



## THE FAINT LIGHT AHEAD

I have had two outright journal acceptances, but they were both co-authored. I co-wrote an article with David Macdonald and Tara Brabazon (2008) and submitted it to *E-Learning* on 14/5/2008. This article was accepted for publication less than three months later on 1/8/2008 (without any substantial changes being required before moving to copy editing for minor stylistic changes thought desirable). It was published in the third issue of the 2008 volume.

Another outright success was an article that also was co-authored, with Leonie Rowan and Julianne Lynch (2006). It was submitted to *Studies in Media and Information Literacy Education* and was also accepted without any changes required within a short timeframe (as I recall it was less than eight weeks). From what I have heard and read, these experiences are rarities.

Does this mean I should write more with other authors? Probably yes, however, I wrote the PhD myself with excellent support from my supervisors, but my PhD was sole-authored and so I felt a dearth-like need to publish that work successfully in journal articles.

## THE JOURNEY IS THE DESTINATION?

I have heard the mantra that you should publish during your PhD candidature. This I tried to do. I submitted papers from my PhD to three different international conferences explaining that it was a work in progress. Twice my paper (different forms) was rejected. A third time the paper was accepted for poster presentation only, not a paper delivery. In hindsight I can say that the 'third time's a dream' reality was probably reflective of the fact that my arguments and data analysis were underdeveloped. As a reflection of my thinking, my work was not ready for publication. At a qualitative research conference, I had some very juicy questions directed at me during my poster presentation, including the one derived from the keynote speaker's presentation that 'theory should not be placed before research', that is, 'What is your response to having little data?' This of course is subjective as was the keynote's speech, which denigrated post-structuralist and postmodern views of the world.

The premise remains that 'it is great if you can do it', that is, publish during your PhD. My focus was on completing my PhD, and then while I waited for it to be assessed, I worked on compiling four journal articles. In Chapter 11, Professor Paul Chandler highlights the success he had while publishing his quantitative data during his PhD. In Chapter 13, Professor Jan Wright talks about the pressure to publish during higher degree by research candidature, and the difficulties associated with it, especially if you have solely qualitative data.



## THE OBVIOUS LANDMARK

When I have submitted an article for publication, I have done so believing it was worth publishing. I have followed the instructions for authors regarding text, references, formatting and length. Perhaps what I have not done so well (in hindsight) is analyse the paradigmatic, methodological and analytical values that each journal has. The analysis of these things is crucial to increasing the chances of acceptance and success.

Often, it is easy to be too close to the content of the article or to the project. Having conducted an intensive and extensive study for your PhD, there is no doubt that you may be too close to the content to be able to see the wood for the trees. An example of this was when after two rejections from two different journals about one of the articles I had written from my PhD, my employment supervisor said to me that the article had too many focuses and that I needed to define a new concept in more detail, it was clearly obvious. I thought that by drafting an article, then setting it aside for a few days, then coming back and working on it (and repeating this process many times) it would be enough, but it was not. Of course, you can always spend more time on an article, refining it, crafting it and honing it for its intended audience, but there is a time when you have to say, 'I need feedback and someone else to cast their eyes over it.' This person needs to have a similar mindset to you (theoretically and methodologically) in order to understand what you are doing, but in other cases, it may be better for someone from a different field to read and give feedback on your work. If the text and purpose of the article is clear to somebody else who knows nothing about your research, then your communication is apt.

But if you have done so according to the guidelines synthesised in Chapter 1, for example, checked the argument is coherent, and that the article is methodologically sound, you still may be too 'close' to your work, which will cause your article to still be rejected or further revisions requested. Rejections are common and revisions are ubiquitous, especially if you have not done your homework.

## SEEKING DIRECTION



It remains of crucial importance to have a critical friend with whom you can reciprocate readings and edits of each other's works. Writing with someone else makes this process easier. But if that is not possible, having somebody with whom you can take a manuscript and receive objective feedback is invaluable. However, you cannot rely on others to do the work for you, nor can you expect that others will 'figure it out' for you. They can only provide advice and encouragement.

Many academics present papers at conferences in order to obtain feedback about their work and then further refine the same document for journal submission. While this may prove valuable to some, it seems difficult to argue that a careful reading from an objective colleague who gives constructive feedback is less valuable than a conference presentation. I have been to conferences where the feedback has been little, and the attendees have only shared about their own similar work, not actually making suggestions of how the paper can be improved. Needless to say, if you strongly deem your learning to take place while talking, then conferences are favoured. I myself learn best when writing, therefore my preferred means of communication lies with this forum.

## THE SUCCESSFULLY NAVIGATED PATH

During the course of my PhD, there was an interesting theme that came through the data – that of addiction to computers. I thought it a pertinent topic to write about and consequently, wrote a book proposal entitled, *The Multiplicities of Internet Addiction*, and submitted a book proposal to Ashgate in late 2007. It was accepted early 2008 and the full manuscript was submitted in July 2008 (Johnson 2009a). While I had submitted this proposal to two other publishers, one of whom was very interested yet could not get it past their editorial board, the process of having the proposal accepted and the book contract signed was not a difficult one. In fact, it has been enjoyable. Two reviewers read two of the proposed chapters and offered useful advice, while also expounding enthusiasm for its publication.

Going about crafting a 150-page book was demanding, challenging and satisfying. I tried to make each chapter sit on its own yet be essentially linked to the others. While I was exhausted when I finally submitted the full manuscript, writing the book proved to be immensely gratifying. A journal article, by nature of its genre, is brief (10,000 words is the most I have seen as a maximum, some are only 2,500 words), and can only hint at the context of the research, the history of its development and process of data analysis. It is unsatisfying to write but, for readers, it is very pleasant to get a quick glimpse of others' work in a general synopsis.



Perhaps that is why many academics love to talk about their work so much. When asked about their research, academics inevitably become animated and are thrilled to talk about their endeavours. In journal articles, their work is confined to the word count, whereas conversations can be extensive. That said, the journal article genre will continue to be very much in demand due to its succinct nature and cut-throat conventions (more about this in Chapter 3).

## AM I GOOD ENOUGH?

It seemed that, for me, until I had my articles accepted in a journal that my PhD – while well crafted for my thesis examiners – was not acceptable as a scholarly work. I felt that though my examiners' comments on my thesis were supportive and approving, that unless I received approval from the prestige of academic journals that I was not up to scratch. In my mind, this was because of the following aspects:

- My study was qualitative.
- My study had a small sample (eight participants).
- My study used a French theorist's ideas (Pierre Bourdieu) to frame and analyse the study, definitely an 'abstract, critical theory', therefore my study employed critical theory, deemed by some perhaps to not be scientific.
- I did not have a hypothesis; I had research questions.

- The thesis was written for examiners who would be sympathetic to my positioning within cultural studies.
- My paradigm is postmodern/post-structuralist, an anathema to those who are positivist and post-positivist.
- I am a feminist.

Therefore, to many people, not just academics, my PhD study would be considered as unscientific or as a whole lot of academic waffle due to its 'lack of data'. I say this because people whose work is only quantitative (and therefore positivist or post-positivist) tend to (or can) look down upon those whose work is not. This has been the case since the day dot, well, in fact, since the dawn of 'science'. Research in the humanities and/or qualitative research have been considered 'soft' compared to the 'hard' sciences of mathematics, chemistry and physics. If content is not 'measurable' or 'objective' then it has less value. In addition, Sandra Harding (1986, 1991) and others have suggested that the development of the disciplines of logic, science and technology have been in association with males only, to the detriment of women and their exclusion from these disciplines and their exclusion from the development of logic (Harding 1986; Lloyd 1993; Spender 1995). Connell (1995: 21) explained that, historically:



> *Resistance to women's emancipation was bolstered by a scientific doctrine of innate sex difference. Women's exclusion from universities, for instance, was justified by the claim that the feminine mind was too delicately poised to handle the rigours of academic work. The resulting mental disturbance would be bad for their capacities to be good wives and mothers.*

From the Middle Ages in the initial development of universities, it was believed that just as the female body was weaker than the male's, the female mind was weaker than the male's. Women were discouraged in the pursuit of academic knowledge, for example; traditional Enlightenment theorists denied the potential for objective, scientific thought to be found in females (Morritt 1997).

I wondered if my thesis was any good at all because it took so long to get my journal articles (derived from my thesis) accepted. I really questioned the quality of my intellect and my work because I had not successfully had these articles published. But, what I have come to realise is that wondering, 'Am I good enough?' happens constantly as an academic. This is due in part to the fact we have to be good at everything. Teaching, administration, winning research grants, organising students, managing budgets, employing casual assistants, successfully supervising doctorate students, not to mention successfully publishing articles in refereed journals. So I suggest that it is very common when academics attend and present at conferences, or submit their work to peer review, that by putting their work out there, they are really wondering if what they are doing is any good at all. Only after the affirmation and acceptance of your work can you build up resilience to these feelings. Indeed, I have a colleague who is very serious about her work and does not ever feel inadequate about presenting her work or receiving feedback on her articles she has submitted for review, but she is an experienced researcher and has proven herself amongst academics already. For those of us who are still 'newbies', and who are working mostly by ourselves, and not as part of a collaborative team, we continually second guess ourselves.

Until you have 'PhD' after your name and has established a research profile, this sense of being good enough cannot be attained. Even then, you must remain watchful to continue successful navigation.



## SUCCESS AT LAST?

When I had had two articles (based on my PhD) accepted for publication, I felt more confident. I felt like I had made it. Though they were not published yet at the time of writing (January 2009), to me, it remained an achievement to have had these articles accepted. It seems unreal that the achievement of having your PhD submitted, approved and awarded is an OK result, but that the acceptance of two sole-authored articles in academia seems superior. Now, if these articles were accepted by prestigious journals (that is, with an IF of more than 1.0), then my sense of achievement would be even greater. I am learning to carve a path through the jungle, but I acknowledge that surviving this environment is very tough.

Perhaps this is a developmental stage of progress. When you can say, 'Yes, I have published two articles from my thesis', then that is when you say, 'Yes, I know what I am doing.' But no, as I write this at the time of having had two sole-authored articles accepted for what I consider to be high-esteemed journals, I have only a little confidence in the continuation of my articles being accepted.

## TRAVEL IS SLOW

I used to work in a school as a teacher. Things happened quickly. The demand was high. New initiatives would be swiftly implemented. Decisions were made on the spot. Though not all schools operate like this, I have found universities and academia to operate fairly slowly. There seems to be lots of consultation, and a fair amount of bureaucratic red tape that delays plans and their implementation. This correlates to the review and submission of journal articles. No one is paid to review journal articles. Few are paid to edit journals. Reviewers and editors do this role to contribute to the wider academic community and because it looks good on their curriculum vitae when they go for promotion. If reviewers are doing it out of the goodness of their heart (or for their professional development, which is probably a more appropriate reason), it is possible that they are already established and have little time to do the reviewing. Hence, the timeline for the submission and acceptance or rejection of my sole-authored articles has taken more than a year for each article. In the high demand for publications to justify employment, tenure and promotion, the wait is an anguish. The paths taken in the jungle are very slow-going. If a rejection comes after three months to block that path, the way back is also very slow as you rethink the journal audience, the structure of the article, the actual data included in the article, not to mention the stylistic conventions utilised. If a 'please resubmit' is received after six months, another couple of months revising the article is necessary which means that the journey on the path becomes longer. If, as in the case of Article 1, the resubmission is rejected, then retreating backwards along the sorry path can be soul-destroying (though not as much now as I look back on it). Then, there is the continuing path of waiting until an article is published once it is accepted. Sickness, botched administration, email failures, press difficulties and disagreement amongst reviewers all prolong the journey. The final destination of journal article publication is long awaited.



I felt very supported in the faculty where I commenced my career as a full-time academic. However, my colleagues were and are very busy. I do not feel right in asking and expecting others to comment on my articles and papers. It can be difficult to find people who can give you constructive feedback that you trust. Therefore, one option that is open to you in order to obtain this desperately needed feedback, is to submit articles to journals which eventually will get reviewed (and rejected), but you are able to obtain feedback in this way. As I have done this, my writing has consequently improved, and I have developed a tougher, thicker skin in the process. Each time a revision occurs, your writing improves. (I still have a lot to learn, evidenced in the rejection of Article 6.)

## POSTSCRIPT

As this goes to press, I can state that the following have been published from my PhD: one book, one refereed conference paper, and four refereed journal articles. Phew! I have also been promoted to a senior lecturer position at Monash University, Victoria. The hard work has paid off. However, I could have made it much easier for myself. Let me explain how.

# 3 Navigating New Terrain: The Demise of the Book?

The field of humanities debate the merits of books versus journal articles. The weighting of merit is becoming very important in this age of measuring performance and impact. This chapter provides a timely overview of these new developments, synthesising the literature in this area. While there is a move to publish only electronic books (e-books), the place of the hardback or paperback book is in question.

## THE STATUS OF BLOGS AND WIKIS VERSUS JOURNAL ARTICLES AND BOOKS

Tara Brabazon (2008) has criticised the advent of bloggers who claim to be experts simply because they have a blog, or web presence. Some of these social commentators seem to have an inflated sense of worth due to their technological efficacy and daily or regular cyberspace diatribes. Cyberspace enables anyone to set themselves up as an expert, or construct themselves as something other than they are (especially in virtual worlds), but the weight of what has been posted online has to be measured up according to what is valued. For example, we tend to value Reuters reports whether they are published in a newspaper or within an online news forum, but who is to say that their reporting is any less biased than an amateur who tweets on Twitter about their observations of an event?

What does hold the blogs and wikis in good stead is the collaborative sense of ownership and the sharing of knowledge within cyberspace. The status that people have in their real, biological lives is not so prevalent or important in cyberspace as identities are negotiable and represented in various ways (Booth 2008). Blog owners and wiki contributors are having their say and drawing on each other (which makes it more likely that only bloggers are referring to other blogs), but therein lies a strong network that contributes to the wisdom of the crowd (Surowiecki 2004). Blogs are 'heralded as the new guardians of democracy, a revolutionary form of bottom-up news production and a new way of constructing self and doing community in late-modern times' (Hookway 2008: 91). In the same way that schooling as an institution is being challenged and teachers' knowledge is limited, is the status of the university being challenged?

It is possible that you can have a love affair with technology, similar to or more than someone's love affair with books. But the love affairs are different. And I doubt that you can really be in love with both media at the same time. Our efficacy with technology, and the degree to which we have taken it up in our lives, will determine whether we prefer to read 'real' books, or electronic text on a screen. We may indeed have a preference for particular genres in electronic form (Internet news), while we will never read a newspaper. We may always choose to read fictional novels for pleasure, while the task of reading journal articles is one played out on a screen. That said, it is unlikely that the expensive book proudly displayed on the coffee table will be replaced by an e-book *on* a laptop.



## NEGOTIATING THE GENRE

What about publishing your thesis as a book? Websites such as http://port.igrs.sas.ac.uk/about.htm offer some ideas about choosing whether a book or journal articles might be more suitable, but it is not in any way comprehensive or enlightening based on actual academics' narratives. While Ashgate provide a useful three-page document that offers advice about publishing your PhD as a book, there are now publishers that offer to publish theses with little changes from the thesis genre to the book genre (for example, Eburon and VDM Verlag Dr. Muller). This degrades the effectiveness of the book genre. My argument for this statement follows.

Luey (2002) expounds on the differences between the genre of a thesis and the genre of a book. Just as the genres between book and thesis are different, so are the genres between a thesis and journal articles. In writing a book there is freedom. There is scope, open form and limitless direction for an academic who might write a book. There is little restraint. There are few conventions and flexibility is provided within the purpose and focus of the text, as well as the way the book is constructed. Although there is a 'house style' and word length to conform to, the format of a book is basically unique to the author. The genre of the book can have many audiences, can encapsulate formality and informality, and each chapter can vary in purpose. The three approaches in Huff's table (Table 3.1) can each be drawn upon in a book. To me, the genre of the book is expressive, more satisfying, more comprehensive, more thorough and more complete. A book expresses more of a person's voice and opinion and is less influenced by intellectual gatekeepers. There are fewer reviews prior to publication, and there are fewer rules (especially unwritten ones). In a book, the author's subjectivity is highlighted, but the author is positioned as an expert. The book is outward focused, that is, it is focused on contributing to the literature in its field, and has supportive editors who want to see your work published as it is in their best interests.

Writing for a journal is like fitting your work to the conventions of a container. There are walls to accommodate, volume to fill, specifications to meet (see Chapters 1 and 6), little of which is directed when you write an academic book (this does of course depend on the publisher and editor). With a journal, the editor's best interests are in the perpetuation of a high rejection rate in order to promote the esteem of the journal. The genre of a journal article can take various forms but in essence it is brief. Despite this brevity, it reflects your epistemological stance. The journal article has extensive, peculiar conventions and must be vetoed by two or more (compliant) reviewers and an editor. The article must promote the journal's quality and must cite its own previously published articles in order to promote itself. The journal is inward focused, that is, it is focused on the promotion of itself, it praises objectivity and it is clinical in method.



Huff (1999) specifies the various writing alternatives evident in academic writing (Table 3.1).

**Table 3.1 Writing alternatives**

| **Audience** | **Format** | **Purpose** | **Approach** |
|---|---|---|---|
| Close Peers | Formal Paper | Inform | Extend Theory |
| Another Field | Presentation | Persuade | Present Data |
| International | Essay | Describe | Review Literature |
| Academic | | Explore | |
| Practitioner | | | |

*Source*: Huff 1999: 33.

When considering the appropriate medium for publication, we must consider the audience of a genre, which will help to determine its format and its purpose. There tends to be three types of articles – those that review literature (of which few are published), those that present research and those that engage with theory of which they extend. Of course, many articles combine these three aspects. It is very unlikely that any research paper will not be situated within a prior literature review (more in Chapter 5). However, in regard to the journal article, its audience is academic and perhaps international, its format is formal, its purpose negotiable depending on the type of article employed.

## THE WEIGHT OF THE WORK

When I first began my postgraduate study, I read many books. They were my predominant source for information about the fields in which I was interested. Books seem to carry weight, figuratively and literally, as they comprise depth and breadth of thought and scholarship. However, my supervisor informed me of the academic need to read and include journal articles in my literature review because of the fact that journal articles deliver succinct reports of recently conducted research, which have been subject to rigorous peer review. Few books are subject to such scrutiny. But in comparison to the number of books deemed to be 'fundamental reading', few journal articles are considered essential reading, nor are they placed with pride upon an office bookshelf. There are reasons for this phenomena: a) they are always placed amongst other articles in the issue, and b) few journals publish exclusively in print format. It seems that the electronic article and issue carries less weight and is less impressive than a journal that has its entity in print, and a book that represents a real, tactile and comprehensive work. Of course, depending on the field in which you are positioned, books may be more favoured, but as with most things, there is a balance to find and maintain.



While impact factors (IF) and high ratings of journals have their place (see Chapter 6 for details on what these are), online access to articles provides apt distribution of your work. People search by terms, not by journal titles, so for the early career academic, just having your work available in an online forum and indexed in multiple databases can be considered appropriate. Your online contributions can increase your international profile. In pre-computer days, when academics only had access to those journals to which they subscribed and had delivered to their office, they relied more on the title of the journal. The distributed access of online knowledge means that this structure is no longer as valid as it once was.

## THE MOVE TO E-BOOKS

An e-book does not give you the pleasure associated with curling up on the couch, devouring the text and being in a world of your own. A laptop is still an unfriendly, inanimate object, with no life of its own, reliant on the user for its activity. Printed pages have more aesthetic and intrinsic value than the electronic version on a LCD screen. Tactile people love the feel and smell of new (and old) books. Print seems to have a permanency, like it will last forever, whereas digital text is uselessly archived, if at all. Expired digital texts sometimes can no longer be searched for in cyberspace, whereas there is care and funding invested in and associated with public libraries. Amazon Kindle 2 provides a book-like screen where many books and other texts such as blogs can be downloaded so to provide a book-like experience without paper. Will this or the iPad ever replace the fondness we have for the smell of a new book (or an old one), the partiality for touch while turning the pages, and the weakness we have for the sense of bliss we experience in a bookshop?

Deleuze and Guattari (1987) call a book a *little machine* because it is an 'assemblage of different textual forms, times, spaces and bodies of knowledge' (Hickey-Moody 2008: 200). The book comprises years of social practice and of living life. It makes comprehensive connections to itself within the text. To me, the journal article is an even tighter compression of speed, time and place and only represents part of a machine, if it all. Its fine (small) focus and disjointed nature – it is usually, though not always, unrelated to the other articles within the issue and it represents a limited part of your research and your life – means that it can only operate as a part of a machine. The journal article has limited connections as it is meant to stand alone, and it does so in the raw.



When the Internet arrived, predictions arose of how the book would become an artefact of the past. Bookshop business owners were quivering with fear. Newspapers and magazine companies began to question their place on the newsstands. Sales were expected to fall. What has occurred is that consumers are becoming more discerning about what they will read. There are now a lot more choices, and many more media texts that are accessible. Many (digital insiders) prefer online content. However, what remains obvious is that countless people like the tactile experience of turning pages, and sitting at a table, a recliner or on a couch while they read. Living life, and the particular experience of reading text, is not as satisfying when living and reading in front of a (small or large) screen. The smell of print, the feel of paper and the comfort of analogue reading are notable pleasures in life.

The hard-edged, electronic object made up of many unknown materials has its place as an object that opens up cyberspace, but it does not provide the aesthetic, tactile and pleasurable qualities that are evident in browsing in a bookstore, perusing a book or magazine, or sitting down in your favourite chair 'curled up with a book'. My father was correct when he stated he thought that bookshops would not be phased out, because people like to shop, and they like to peruse a book before they buy, and they like to feel the object of interest in their hand.

While e-books are becoming more popular, they seem to sit alongside hardbacks in terms of academic merit, as the hardbacks are filed in the library shelves, but the electronic option is also available in the online databases. This creates flexibility as readers can choose the form of media they engage with.

## NEW WAYS TO NAVIGATE

Luey (2002) devoted 11 pages in her book to the differences between a thesis as a genre and an academic book as a genre, so it is surprising to see the abrupt turnaround and recent (European) popularity of publishing a thesis as a book. To me, this means that neither genre is respected for its conventions, purpose and audience. By converting one into the other, we lessen the value of both. She highlighted how 30–40 years ago, academics did publish their dissertation as a book and it was an accepted practice, perhaps even an important part of obtaining tenure (a permanent position). If you really think your thesis should be published as a book, I would encourage you to read Luey's text as well as *The Thesis and the Book* (Harman et al. 2003), which further argues in detail the differences between these genres.

Luey suggests that if you are bored with your thesis or it has caused you much pain, then you should leave it alone. My perspective is that all your effort should not go to waste and that your dissertation should be reworked to suit the purposes, style and audience of a journal, if not a book. Luey clarified that there are three options – forget it, turn it into a book through extensive revision, or extract one or more articles from it (2002: 36).

There are important questions to ask. Do you have enough new ideas to write a book? Do you have some ideas (findings) that are worth publishing in articles? 'If there is an idea there, how much needs to be said about it – 20 pages or 200? In other words, do you have an article to write, or a book?' (Luey 2002: 38). In the continuum between the thesis genre and the book genre, Luey claims that you may either need a 'cosmetic cover-up', 'limited remodeling' or a 'complete overhaul' (40–41) in order to change your thesis text into a book which has differences in audience, tone, style, context, focus and organisation. Luey suggests putting your thesis on the shelf for a few months once written to give yourself a break, and promote objectivity about something to which you have been so close. You may decide you do not want to publish it, or it is not worth publishing, or you may just hate it. This last scenario is dismaying, but as I have already met a number of early career academics who want nothing more to do with their theses, I am sure it is not uncommon. Now, if you are in the situation where you think your thesis is not worth publishing, there are a number of questions that come to mind. Is it possible that you are going through a poor state of mental health? Perhaps you need to reassess the quality of your thesis at a later date. Perhaps you also need to ask a colleague for their input and help about what parts to publish (or perhaps your supervisor/advisor will assist you). If your PhD is truly not worth publishing, then I must ask why was your PhD awarded? There must have been a significant and original contribution to research and knowledge, otherwise your doctorate would not have been conferred.

## HIERARCHY OF GENRES



Kenway, Gough and Hughes (1998) claimed the following weighting of merit for forms of academic publication within the fields of humanities and social sciences. In order of importance:

1. authored research book published by a commercial press;
2. authored book (other) published by a commercial press;
3. edited book published by a commercial press;
4. book chapter, or refereed article in scholarly journal;
5. article-length review essays;
6. conference papers in refereed proceedings;
7. edited volume of conference proceedings;
8. papers in non-refereed proceedings;
9. non-refereed articles, letters, notes and abstracts;
10. multimedia, that is, newspapers, magazines, radio, TV, documentaries, newsletters, media reports about your research (though may have other benefits). (1998: 11)

In 2010, it seems that with the frequent advent of discourses surrounding what are considered to be 'quality' publications, the refereed article in the scholarly journal, which can be 'measured' through citations and consequent IF, seems to have moved up the scale. 'As a cultural object ... the journal article is intimately connected to both producers and consumers of scholarly knowledge' (Carolan 2008: 70). On the other hand, the sciences have a different hierarchy; a refereed article in a scholarly journal has the highest merit. Many of these journal articles are co-written by numerous authors.

What we do need to consider is what place in the hierarchy the e-book has. Many commercial presses publish e-books alongside hardbacks. They have not yet moved to only publishing e-books. Some e-books are published by organisations similar to Research Online (see http://ro.uow.edu.au/), though it is not a commercial press, but an online repository. Seeing your work in print and holding it in your hand makes you feel like a 'real' author. In 2010, I cannot help thinking that by only publishing an e-book, it would not create this same sense of satisfaction.

In seeking to cut costs, journal publishers have moved to only publish electronic issues. The print version of journals is becoming less available. Practicalities come to mind such as the fact that you cannot/should not make notes on library copies of a journal so photocopies of the article are made anyway. So it seems it is becoming less of a concern to have print copies made available. Obtaining an electronic copy of a journal article that specifically interests you and then printing it if you want to write on it is preferable.

Where does the place of professional journals lie? This depends on whether the journal is peer reviewed. If not, then articles published in that form probably fit alongside the 'non-refereed articles' (number 9 of Kenway et al.'s 1998 list; see above).

## NEW CONCEPTS FOR NEW TIMES

Common Ground Publishing has introduced a new way of publishing conference papers and journal articles. With the associated conference that you attend either in person or virtually, you can submit your paper for blind review in order for it to be published in the yearly volume of its associated journal. Your paper that you present at the conference is not published as a conference paper, but as a refereed journal article. For more information, visit Common Ground (2010).

Common Ground Publishing also organise the International Conference on the Book (see Common Ground 2008) which provides a forum for participants in the book publishing industry, librarians, researchers and teachers from around the world to discuss the past, present and future of the book, and with it, other key aspects of the information society, including publishing, libraries, information systems, literacy and education.

In his text, *Digitize This Book! The Politics of New Media, or Why We Need Open Access Now*, Gary Hall (2008) discusses digitisation, open access, authority and the legitimacy of knowledge. The changing nature of what it means to publish and the authority to which it is aligned continues to be negotiated.

## WEIGHING UP THE MERIT OF THE PUBLICATION

It is a great achievement to write a book. It represents a comprehensive effort that typically has a broader focus than does a journal article. There is no doubt that it is a significant achievement. As shown in Chapter 2, it can be challenging to have your work published in a journal. Having an article not only published in a journal but in a prestigious one is also significant. The conventions of the academic field highlight that there is more difficulty in publishing via these forums than via blogs or microblogs (for example, Twitter). What you have to consider is whether you want the impact of known, quality publications or whether you are happy to appeal to a wide, broad audience where, if taken up, the publication can be more immediate (essays, reflections on your blog for instance).



An interesting anecdote I can share is when I was online talking to an acquaintance who had mentioned that she would like to read my first book. Unfortunately, how the book is priced puts it out of the reach of many people. Her response when finding out the recommended retail price, said, 'Why don't you just blog?' I replied, 'I do!', but, as your ravings on a blog are not submitted to any form of review before publication, they are therefore unlikely to ever have the same status of 'quality' publications in 'quality' media.

In terms of joint authored publications, being the first author is important. As Wilma Vialle refers to in Chapter 14, some take the approach of being alphabetical which can be disappointing if your family name features further down the alphabet. Being a third or fourth author is great to have as a publication, but what counts more is if your name is first (note, this is not the case in all academic fields). When having your publications verified for funding purposes, you have to state the percentage of authorship. This can be advantageous if you have only contributed 20 per cent to an article and yet you have obtained another publication. But if you are first author, no one knows the percentage (unless it is stated), but yet the article is known in academic circles by the first author. Some authors take turns (for example, Bereiter and Scardamalia; Scardamalia and Bereiter). While having any (print or electronic) publication is good, having a publication in a quality journal is better, and having your name as the first author is even better.

# 4 Flies, Gnats and Wasps: Negotiating the Gatekeepers

What are your chances? This chapter gives recent figures from current editors about the rejection rate, acceptance rate, submission rate and numbers of revisions that are requested. This opens our eyes to how difficult this process is and highlights how 'getting your work out there' in less prestigious journals (perhaps with higher acceptance rates) is possibly a more feasible option.

What the following figures demonstrate is that there are high rejection rates for most journals. Many times, this happens because the type of article submitted does not suit the journal's focus. What you should remember is that you will receive more rejections than acceptances, and that you increase your chances of acceptance if you thoroughly profile suitable journals and specifically write for a journal in mind.

This is the email I sent to approximately 50 journal editors:

> *To the Editor,*
>
> *I am writing a book entitled 'Publishing from Your PhD: Negotiating a Crowded Jungle'. As part of the research for this book, I wish to obtain recent figures from your journal's submission, reviewing and publishing process. I am writing to ask you the following questions:*
>
> *In the past calendar year, how many articles have been submitted to your journal for review? How many articles were rejected outright? How many articles were asked to be resubmitted? How many articles were published?*
>
> *If you have percentages rather than figures available for the past calendar year or previous years, that would also be appreciated.*

> *This information will be made publicly available in my published book. I trust you are happy to provide these details. Thank you in advance.*
>
> *Kind regards,*
>
> *Nicola*

I had close to a 50 per cent response rate from these busy academics. Several journal editors replied stating that they were unable to give permission for the requested information. Comments I received pertaining to this response were along the lines of, 'the other statistics you require remain a matter of Editorial and Publisher confidentiality' and 'the journal's policy is not to provide this information'.



What follows below are direct quotes from the emails I received from journal editors (in no particular order). Quite a few journal editors replied by stating that their publication did provide similar information within their editorials. As can be gleaned from my email (above), by replying to my email and providing figures about their journal, they were consenting to have these figures published in this book.

❖❖❖

*International Review of Qualitative Research* The Editor, Norman Denzin, replied:

> *We are a young journal, barely a year old. We have published 30 articles (half were solicited). We had 85 submissions the first year, with a 95% rejection rate. We asked for four articles to be revised and resubmitted.*

❖❖❖

*Educational Studies* Ian White, Publisher, Journals (Education), Routledge/Taylor & Francis, replied:

> *The acceptance rate for Educational Studies is around the 30–35% mark. This statistic having been derived from the number of papers published/number of papers received in the calendar year from Jan to end Dec-08.*

*If you care to take a look at the journal's website (www.tandf.co.uk/edstudies), the number of articles published in 2008 can be seen from there. The journal is included in the ISI Social Sciences Citation Index (education, educational research category) and boasts an impact factor of 0.246 which ranks it at 89/105.*

*I'm afraid that the other statistics you require remain a matter of Editorial and Publisher confidentiality.*

❖❖❖

*Journal of Computer-Mediated-Communication* The Editor, Kevin Wright, replied:

*Last year we received 320 submissions to JCMC. About 7% of these articles were rejected because they were either inappropriate for the journal (i.e. a focus on engineering aspects of computers) or they had other problems (i.e. a sample of 5 participants, etc.). For 34% of the articles, the authors were given the chance to revise and resubmit the manuscript. 40 manuscripts were accepted for publication, and the rest were rejected or are still being processed. We have a 16% acceptance rate.*



❖❖❖

*Fast Capitalism* The Editor, Ben Agger, replied:

*The data are somewhat sketchy. We don't keep track but I have an impressionistic sense. We solicit many pieces and a bunch are submitted to us unsolicited. I'd say that we accept about 20% of the unsolicited submissions; it might actually be lower than that. The vast majority of the unsolicited ones that we reject have two problems, sometimes at the same time: they are intellectually beyond the scope of our journal and we recommend that they be submitted elsewhere, and/or they are not well-done. In the past year we have put out two issues and these have included 28 articles. Of all the papers that we accept (including both solicited and unsolicited ones), I'd say that about 50% are not accepted outright but are sent back for revision. We work a lot with authors in polishing their work. It has also become clear to us that by the fourth year of our journal's existence, we have reached a tipping point and we now receive many unsolicited submissions.*

*One more point: we publish both well-known senior people and less well-known junior people, including people who are working on their diss[ertation] or have just completed it. We pride ourselves on this mix of junior and senior contributors.*

*All work submitted is refereed–read by at least two people and sometimes more. Unless it is totally outside the ballpark of the journal, which does happen, as I said above.*

❖❖❖

*Computers & Education* The Editor, Rachelle Heller, replied to the following two questions:

*In the past calendar year, how many articles have been submitted to your journal for review? Somewhere over 700.*



*How many articles were rejected outright? Our accept[ance] rate is about 23%.*

❖❖❖

*Journal of Computing in Teacher Education* The Associate Editor, Denise Lindstrom, replied:

*For the calendar year of 2008,*

*Submitted: 42*
*Editorial Decline: 8*
*Reviewer Decline: 15*
*Pending Revisions: 2*
*Pending Review: 8*
*Published: 9*

❖❖❖

*British Journal of Educational Technology* The Editor, Nick Rushby, replied:

*Unfortunately I only have detailed information for the calendar year 2008.*

*In that 12-month period we received 311 manuscripts for peer review and a further 40 colloquium submissions. About 50% of the colloquia were accepted.*

*Of the 311 submissions for peer review only one was accepted without revision. About 20% were accepted after revision. Taking the peer reviewed and colloquia together, the overall acceptance rate was 32.7%.*

*Subjectively, the percentages for 2007 were similar with a slightly small[er] number of submissions.*

*We shall probably have to reduce the acceptance rate this year because the size of the printed journal is fixed and limits the number of papers we can publish. As the submission numbers increase then we have to be more selective on quality.*



❖❖❖

*International E-Journal of Elementary Education* The Editor, Turan Temur, replied:

*IEJEE is a peer-reviewed electronic journal.*

*It's a multidisciplinary journal with main emphasis on teaching and learning issues within the area of elementary education. Also IEJEE is a very young journal in elementary education as you know. In the past calendar year and at the first issue; submitted: 12 articles, 1 book review. Sum: 13*

*Rejected: 9*
*Re-submitted: 3 (these articles were published also)*
*Published: 3*
*Book review: 1*

❖❖❖

*Australasian Journal of Educational Technology* The Editor, Roger Atkinson, directed me to the *Australasian Journal of Educational Technology* website (AJET 2008) for the information I was seeking, which also appeared in Atkinson and McLoughlin (2008). From 2003–2007, the percentage of acceptance rates ranged from 21.3%–33%.

❖❖❖

*The Qualitative Report* The Editor, Ronald Chenail, replied:

> *Nicola,*
>
> *Your book sounds quite interesting! Many of our authors are first time authors and many of them are attempting to publish the findings from their qualitative research dissertation.*
>
> *We try not rejecting any papers as long as the subject matter is qualitative research in nature. We want to help authors publish their work so our approach is one of mentoring (see http://www.nova.edu/ssss/QR/Editorial/editstm.html for more on our editorial approach).*
>
> *You can find information about The Qualitative Report's submissions and acceptance rates by going to http://www.nova.edu/ssss/QR/numbers.html where we have posted our statistics for the last seven years. If you have any questions, please let me know and best of luck with your book!*
>
> *Ron*

❖❖❖

[I then accessed the suggested website and retrieved the information below (accessed 10 February 2009).

> *Since January 2002 we have received 678 original manuscripts from authors living in the United States, Puerto Rico, and 50 other nations from around the world. Even though we accept more than 89% of these authors who submit their papers to TQR for inclusion in our manuscript development process, we end up publishing slightly more than 36% of their papers in the journal. This lower publication rate reflects the rigorous editorial development program each author must successfully complete before our editors and board deem their papers ready for publication. Papers published in TQR therefore represent exemplary hard work and positive collaboration on the part of our authors, editors, and reviewers.*

❖❖❖

*International Journal of Emerging Technologies and Society* The Managing Editor, Sue Malta, replied:

*As we are currently investigating publication possibilities with academic publishing houses, we are unable to supply you with all the information you require. We can, however, tell you that for 2008 the overall rejection rate for articles was 60%.*

❖❖❖

*British Educational Research Journal* The Co-Editors of BERJ (Christine Skelton and Gary Thomas) provided the following detailed information.

*From previous administration to 17th August 2008*

| **Articles in system at 31st December 2007** | **37** |
|---|---|
| | |
| *Articles rejected after review* | *12* |
| *In process* | *12* |
| *Accepted* | *10* |
| *Static* | *3* |

*January 2008–31st May 2008*

| **Articles submitted between 1st January and 31st May 2008** | **81** |
|---|---|
| | |
| *Reject at stage 1:* | *45* |
| *Reject at stage 2: (after being sent for review)* | *11* |
| *Withdrawn* | *1* |
| *In process* | *21* |
| *Accept after minor revisions* | *1* |
| *Accepted* | *1* |
| **1 submission broke protocol by sending article to two journals at the same time* | *1* |
| *Total* | *81* |

*17th May–17th August 2008*

| ***Articles submitted from May to 17th August 2008*** | ***74*** |
|---|---|
| | |
| *Awaiting initial decision* | *12* |
| *Reject at stage 1* | *23* |
| *Reject at stage 2: (after being sent for review)* | *1* |
| *In process (includes papers awaiting reviewer agreement)* | *38* |
| | |
| *Total* | *74* |

*August 2008–February 2009*



*At the end of August we had 21 articles in process. We have accepted 11 of those, 3 were rejected after review and 9 are currently ongoing.*

❖❖❖

*Studies in Higher Education* The Editor, Malcolm Tight, replied:

> *Studies in Higher Education is a widely cited, internationally recognised and competitive journal to publish in, currently receiving about eight times as many articles as it can publish. While this may seem off-putting, we do aim to provide all authors with helpful feedback, and many that we reject are subsequently revised and published elsewhere.*
>
> *About 20% of the material we receive is rejected after an initial editorial review. A further 65% or so is rejected after careful review, with the authors receiving a full account of the reasons for rejection and a copy of the referees' comments. We proceed with the remaining 15% or so of articles, which will invariably require some revision or further work, most of which will subsequently be published.*

❖❖❖

*Teaching and Teacher Education Qualitative Research* Sara Delamont, Editor of both, provided the following information:

*Teaching and Teacher Education gets 600 papers submitted every year compared to 80–90 for Qualitative Research.*

❖❖❖

*Australian Journal of Education* The Editor, Glenn Rowley, replied:

*In 2008, exactly 100 articles were submitted. Of these, 44 were rejected outright, 25 were rejected following a full review process, 22 were asked to revise and resubmit, 20 were ultimately published, 8 are still in process and one was withdrawn by the author.*

*Please bear in mind that I became Editor in March 2008, so these figures involve my interpretation of information in files that I inherited.*

*Also, the information records the fates (to the extent that they are known) of articles actually submitted during 2008. We would normally publish 18 articles in a year (6 per issue). The 20 acceptances include some that have appeared (or will appear) in 2009. The 18 that were actually published in 2008 includes some that were submitted in 2007.*



❖❖❖

*New Zealand Journal of Educational Studies* The Editor, Liz Gordon, replied:

*In [the] 2008 year, 37 papers were submitted to the NZJES. Of those*

*4 were sent back without review*
*9 were reviewed and declined*
*2 were withdrawn*
*3 were requested for resubmission*
*16 were or are to be published*

*The rest are still under revision.*

❖❖❖

All replies received from editors were thanked, even if policy did not permit them to provide me with the information I sought. One of the editors replied to the original request, 'A minority of articles are rejected without being sent out for review. The great majority are rejected after review, with only a minority proceeding further on to possible publication.'

I hope you are able to take some comfort from the fact that many journals have a high rejection rate. Journals need to have a narrow scope so they can make a name for themselves in their field. They are competitive and wish to appear scholarly and reputable. The need to build their profile and have high standards. They are not going to publish anything that does not support these goals. The editors, the editorial boards and the reviewers are the gatekeepers that are also working towards these goals.

Based on this information, submitting an article to a lesser-known journal, or a young journal does not necessarily increase your chances of acceptance. In addition, submitting to a journal that has more issues per year (per volume), does not mean that the acceptance rate is higher. Not submitting your article to a journal that has hundreds of submissions per year, in preference for one that has less than a hundred submissions each year, does not mean that your chances of acceptance increase. Some journal editors are noting huge increases in their submission rate because they recently have been highly ranked by external organisations. As the measurement of output and impact is becoming more important, so is the quality of where work is published. If journal article submissions increase, but there is only space for 24 articles per year to be published, then not only might the acceptance rate be affected, but the delay from acceptance to publication may be longer.



What else is also interesting is that many articles in the system are taking a long time to be published, because of resubmission, revision and editing requirements. This highlights the need to be patient with the typically long process. It also suggests that you can increase the speed of acceptance by making sure your journal article is exemplary in its spelling, punctuation, grammar and flow.

The provision of this information is not meant to be comprehensive. It is meant to provide information that will help you to be realistic about the likelihood of acceptances. It also emphasises that much effort is required in order to seek out the 'right' journal for your work and submit your article according to its conventions and peculiarities. How to do this is detailed in Chapter 6.

# 5 The Night is Black: No Black or White in Academia

This chapter attempts to discuss how preferences for different paradigms are published in different journals. In this chapter, notions of the various approaches about what is deemed 'publishable' or not are dispelled. As what is deemed publishable in one journal is an anathema in another, explanation of paradigm, methodological and ideological wars are brought to light.

## BEWARE OF FASCISTS ON YOUR PATH: THE MEANING OF THEORY

The concept of 'theory' means different things to different people. Craswell clarified this issue when he stated:

> *Theories are abstract systems in which certain aspects (the key ideas or principles of a theory) are privileged by an author over other possibilities. Theorists abstract from the chaotic, actual world of everyday events and activities that which they consider most significant to explain that world, or some aspect of it. Theories are useful for their explanatory value, and perhaps their predictive value. They can open up different possibilities in ways of perceiving and understanding complex events and happenings important in your context of academic enquiry, and so prove to be valuable tools of analysis. (2005: 34–5)*

That said, there are different aspects of theory. For instance, a theoretical framework is where you might 'explain and perhaps justify the choice of an existing body of theory being applied by you, or set up and expound on a framework you are constructing from a range of different theories' (Craswell 2005: 35). An analytical framework will 'detail and expound on the parts of the analysis as well as the logical relations among those parts, or propose a model for analysis of data, which may involve addressing theoretical issues' (2005, 35). Whereas a conceptual framework might 'outline the general notions or themes being engaged in the research and expound on the logical relations among those. This too may involve dealing with theory' (2005: 35).

An obvious statement that Cantor makes (which I wish I knew how obvious it was many years ago), was that there are three kinds of journal articles:

1. reports of empirical research or qualitative studies;
2. review articles;
3. philosophical arguments or theoretical articles. (Cantor 1993: 45)



It is evident that some academics with pragmatic paradigms do not view theoretical articles as 'real' research and may actually term them as 'creative writing'. This is despite the comprehensive application of an apt metaphor that might enhance the way you think about a concept. These philosophical discussions, while complicated and theoretical, are not viewed by some to be real research and, indeed, some do not claim to be research as such. Though a fair amount of literature reviewing may have been done, and though the depth of engagement in theory is notable, many people view this kind of article to be 'academic waffle'. The intensity of the scholarly engagement is negated by those who say 'real' research is only that which is collected and analysed – that data is publishable. Journals that publish highly theoretical or conceptual papers are not the best vehicle for pragmatic, straightforward papers. While it can be easy to 'box' journals into either the 'highly theoretical' category or the 'pragmatic' category, it can be harder to determine those journals that will publish both, because they tend to like a 'bit of both' in their volumes. Indeed, my articles are positioned at neither end of the continuum, and two articles I had accepted from my PhD were published in what are known as 'comprehensive' journals, that is, journals that cover a wide range of educational issues regarding research in education. Most journals in education tend to be more specific and focus on subcategories of education such as educational psychology, higher education, early childhood, mathematics and so on.

Review articles can be comments on other articles or research, or could possibly include reviews about literature. As Professor Jan Wright (in Chapter 13) comments, these types of articles are becoming harder to publish. One reason is that they are difficult to write to a high standard, and another reason is that they do not contribute anything 'new'. To write and comment on previously or currently published research (that is, in the same article), it is likely you would have to be specifically invited, or be one of the reviewers who wished to formally comment on the article.

Some journals also have 'research notes' which are shorter reports on empirical research. Many of them are works in progress, or updates on work completed.

## THE PATHS ARE BLOCKED: DIFFERENT REQUIREMENTS FOR DIFFERENT PATHS

It is common to get contrary reviews, or what seem like discrepant reviews. Contrasting reviews tend to focus on different things or want different types of analyses to come through. You cannot give what you do not have, and sometimes a reviewer cannot see beyond his or her own perspective, or take on the world, so it is such that they may really not understand what it is you are trying to say, and what limitations you have on the work. What you should know is that what some reviewers like will be disliked by other reviewers.



You can always make yourself feel inadequate. In academia, it is an easy thing to do. There is always something else you can read; a literature review is never complete. There is always something else you can research, or something else that could be included. But you have to come to the point where you say, while this work has limitations, it is worthy of publication. Then the long process of waiting for reviews to come back begins.

Why do reviews take so long? As stated before, reviewers and editors are doing this job because of their commitment to the profession. It is not part of their normal day-to-day job. For an editor, they require time to check that first, an article is worth being sent out for review, second, they assign appropriate reviewers, third, chase up busy reviewers for their reports, and fourth, sometimes mediate conflicting reviews, or summarise the reviews in general. If reviewers are conscientious to meet deadlines, then a quick turnaround may be possible, but in the possible event of sickness, catastrophe, high stress and overwork, the review of your article may be at the bottom of the agenda.

There are people and academics who can appreciate the diversity and perspectives of differing methodologies. But, there are methodological fascists who only value the type of work they do. Beware, and be prepared to acknowledge this inherent bias if it is evident, and do not be perturbed if you are the target of a cruel review. Resubmit again requesting another reviewer or resubmit to an alternative avenue. Promise yourself and in your response to other up-and-coming academics that you will never be so close-minded that you can neither consider nor appreciate the benefits of a paradigmatic approach that contrasts with your own. Whether you have a love affair with statistics, action research or the use of metaphors to illuminate how to think about findings, you need to know why it is you value what you do, and what and why other perspectives or paradigms will not value or heavily criticise what you do.

## A LIGHT (GUIDELINE) FOR ONE PATH

When submitting a paper for review to one of their numerous conferences and associated journals, Common Ground Publishing asks that you stipulate whether your paper has a practice focus, a research focus or a theory focus. This means that reviewers are able to consider the paper in light of the focus, rather than in light of their beliefs about what constitutes good research. The following quotation explains the different categories, which provides a useful framework to consider other articles:



> ***Practice Focus:*** *A paper which describes innovative or exemplary practices or programs in the community, in workplaces, in education institutions and the like. This may take the form of case studies, narratives, demonstrations or technical reports. The outcomes of practice may be improved frameworks, concepts, understandings or structures, such as enhanced capacity through the development of skills, knowledge and operational effectiveness. This kind of work may involve putting theory and research into practice.*
>
> ***Research Focus:*** *A presentation or publication reporting upon original research, based on the systematic collection and analysis of data or facts. This kind of work may involve the application or testing of theory.*
>
> ***Theory Focus:*** *A presentation or publication which is broad and generalising in its emphasis, reflecting upon and systematically referenced against one or more bodies of literature or systems of thought. (Common Ground 2010)*

This is an interesting way to frame different approaches. It also helps demarcate and delineate the scope of the paper, and explicitly lets you as the reader know what you are reading about.

## UNDERSTANDING A PATHWAY

Another perspective or example of how different perspectives influence the predominance of grey in academia, is how some academics believe that you should state the limitations of the research study you have conducted, while others believe that it is obvious, or that instead you should state the strengths. The use of the word 'limitations' stems from positivism, so those people who value that paradigm probably will wish for limitations of a study to be included.

Similarly, another area that demonstrates the application of paradigms is whether there is a section that should be included about 'areas for future research' or the 'applications of your findings'. These can be considered to be applications of pragmatic or transformative paradigms, but perhaps demonstrate positivistic tendencies. Additionally, is this the purpose(s) of the article? By not including it, is it a weakness, or, by not including it, are you focusing on a different purpose? You have to be considerate of where you are publishing and why, and what it is that you are valuing by submitting work to particular journals.



## THE NATURE OF THE CROWDED JUNGLE

If you decide to focus on publishing and making a name for yourself in academia, you will surely find that the jungle is crowded. There are many people competing for the available journal article positions in the limited number of issues produced each year. There are many people competing for the available research funds. In addition, you need to be able to argue for why your research is unique as the chances are that it has been done before. The advent of technology within society means that there are continually different avenues opening up for exploration. And of course, we cannot ignore that knowledge is exponentially increasing or doubling regularly. But what counts as knowledge? That is what you have to define for yourself and, with that in mind, set out to publish in journals that also agree with your particular mindset.

A recently retired professor I know once said to me that it pays to get your ideas out there quickly, especially for feedback – the Internet provides this immediate facility. About 15 years ago, he was mulling over some ideas to publish, but Sherry Turkle and Seymour Papert beat him to it (both famous for their work in computers and education). This draws attention to the fact that it is unlikely that your work is particularly original. Somewhere, someone else in the world is probably working on the very same thing as you. That is why you need to do your research or 'homework'. You need to know who else is doing what, and why, and what their angle is, and be prepared to ensure that your work complements or contrasts with what others are doing so that you can claim some originality. This is not assuming that you are trying to replicate what others have done, or plagiarise them. It is just that it is unlikely that what you perceive to be your exciting ideas are anything original. You have to acknowledge that there are always smarter people out there, some who have more time on their hands and some who have more resources at their disposal, so it is continually going to be a competition not only to publish your research, but also to be the first to do so. Consider using a blog and Internet discussion forums to test out your ideas. Do not keep them to yourself and wait until they are perfect before you publish them. The ideas will never get published, or someone else will beat you to it, and then you will have nothing to state as being unique.

You may be asked, does it really matter where you publish? Online access provides apt diffusion so you will be picked up through search keywords, not journal names. In pre-computer days, only precious subscriptions to highly esteemed print journals mattered. While the merits of uploading your lectures on YouTube are dubious (see Brabazon 2009a), the use of blogs and postings that encourage comment from other academics and laypersons means that your work can be reviewed and you can receive that all-important feedback, and you are also able to claim validity and possible originality via the dates of which you have published postings within cyberspace. This is also why you need to get your work published – so that you can be known for the great work that you have done, not someone else in a different country who had a similar idea.

That said, many people, as I have alluded to before, just find the whole thought of publishing overwhelming. They do not know where to start. They may have made the most (or not much) out of publishing from their PhD, but they do not have any new projects to get stuck into, or they are struggling to generate ideas for new writing or new research funding.[1] Others who have tried to publish their work have realised how difficult it is. They are disappointed with discrepant reviews. They are disillusioned with brutal rejections. And they do not share their experiences with others because it remains to be seen as a weakness or a failure if they have not progressed to publishing successfully. But this is not the case! All successful academics (whether they are professors or not) have had failures and disappointments. They have submitted articles to the 'wrong' journals. They have anguished over why their research grant applications were not awarded. They have

1 This is where I highly recommend Boden, Kenway and Epstein's six-volume Academic's Support Kit, as mentioned earlier.

despised themselves for thinking they were on to a 'sure thing'. There is nothing that is guaranteed, especially considering ongoing changes in political climates. Some have published work that they are not particularly proud of, or work that they would rather forget. But they have moved on. They have made the most of their opportunities, and they have been clever and strategic about the paths they have taken, and the effort they have put into hacking that path. Many of them have also been well supported by more experienced academics who have supported them in their efforts to navigate the crowded jungle.

There are others with similar experiences to you, who are also seeking to navigate the crowded jungle. They may be similar in age, gender, previous career changes, writing ability, drive, motivation, intellect, skill sets and dispositions. So, while you are not alone, there is an interesting juxtaposition that lies here. Only you can navigate your own jungle, but you may choose to do so with co-authors and a team of academics. Co-authoring and collaboration has its benefits. But if you have not found that sense of a 'team', then the responsibility for reaching the intended destination in your jungle rests solely on you.



Not everyone will wish to share their embarrassing failures. In fact, many never will. They might pretend to laugh at this manuscript because the very idea of things not being 'rosy' insults their intellect and their ability to succeed.

## THE GREY OF ACADEMIA AND ITS SUBJECTIVITY

You cannot rely on a sense of objectivity or impartiality. Really, it comes down to the particular aims and scope of the journal, whether they consider your data set to be 'big' enough, whether they consider your theoretical contribution to be substantial enough, and whether they wish to be associated with your work. There are many variables that would put editorial boards off from publishing particular results if they may have negative spinoffs from doing so. Editors and editorial boards are obliged to raise the profile and status of the journal of which they are fronting. They are unlikely to go out on a limb to publish some unusual or unique research that is against the norm or against the grain unless it has been extremely well supported in prior lengthy debates. It is possible, but jobs, promotion, tenure, salaries and status are at stake.

What counts as a 'good' article to one journal may be an abhorrence to another. This does not necessarily mean that a journal is lesser than another, but it does mean that they may have a different set of criteria by which they are measuring articles. It could be considered to be differences in perceptions of quality, but it could be considered that there are various beliefs about what constitutes 'good' research and 'good' academic writing, what the value of 'interesting' research or lines of thought has, and how interested the editor is in having that type of work published.

Journals that are seeking to establish themselves may take more risks, but usually they prefer to publish rigorously reviewed work that has been enhanced and crafted since its first submission. They may not have a lot of articles to choose from – perhaps – but they may be looking for more interesting or alternative research projects than what is published in the A-star journals. Regardless of the journal's ranking, you cannot submit the findings of an excellent research project within poorly written material and expect it to be accepted.



So, *opinion* and subjectivity of what is considered to be 'good' is what reigns. Certain people will argue that 'good' research will get published, but it remains that only if others think that it is good, and that it is well written and well presented, will it get published. You cannot submit a half-hearted effort and expect success. There are limitations with any way that research is conducted, and that is why there is such an abundance of different approaches. Naturally, there are moves towards conducting different methods in order to continue improving and enhancing the ways we understand and construct knowledge. Webb, Schirato and Danaher defined subjectivity as, 'a perspective asserting that social reality is produced through the thoughts, decisions and actions of individual agents' (2002: xv). In this version, subjectivity is intertwined with relativity; thus, it is considered to be biased and based on opinion. We all have biases in our position and dispositions (Bourdieu, Chamboredon and Passeron 1991). LiPuma argued there are 'no forms of knowledge and understanding that are not a product of position and position taking within a social field' (1993: 22). Pierre Bourdieu claimed that no one can truly be objective, even with science, as producing scientific texts was inherently political (see LiPuma 1993). Simply, you always risk imposing your 'objective' account upon others.

Reflexivity offers a means of detecting social assumptions (subjectivity) in a way that helps to build up objectivity (see Harding 1992, cited in Hesse-Biber and Leckenby 2004: 219). An additional facet and emphasis of reflexivity is:

> *Not only to inquire into the efficacy and formal rigour of the available theories and methods but also to question the methods and theories at the very moment at which they are implemented, in order to determine*

*what they do to objects and what objects they make. (Bourdieu, Chamboredon and Passeron 1991: 11).*

Therefore, Bourdieu argued for the objectivation of subjectivity, which is a reflexive process by which you reflexively explore the conditions and influences on your subjective construction of objectivity.

So within this grey of academia, you need to identify that some people will value your research and others will not. Particular journals will favour the type of research you do, and others will not. As you may have gathered, the tiers of journals are ranked according to the number of submissions and the opinions that have been submitted. There is continual difficulty in trying to measure quality, and that is why a mix of qualitative and quantitative research tries to congeal richness, specifics, insight and delimiters of findings. But what journals will not accept is poor quality writing that does not adhere to the conventions and style that have been set. If you have interesting work that is written to a high standard that is perhaps different to what a journal normally publishes, then you have a chance. If your work is full with incorrect referencing or UK spelling when American spelling has been requested, then you are setting yourself up for failure and dismissal, despite the blind reviews.



An example of discrepant reviews that I have had to contend with includes what I consider to be minor points and reflections of personal opinions, such as not using personal pronouns, and not citing first names of authors that are referred to within the text. These are minor stylistic conventions that you must clarify before you submit to a journal, but to some people they are despised – they will really get up a reviewer's nose. To give an example from one submission, one reviewer suggested I exclude Bourdieu's conceptual framework completely from the paper, alongside another reviewer's comment on the same paper that Bourdieu's theoretical framework could be more thoroughly linked to the context of the research. In the same article, the first reviewer suggested I have less theoretical analysis but more emphasis on the substantive material in its own right, while the second suggested I include more data analysis in light of the theory.[2]

As Professor Lori Lockyer points out in Chapter 12, while it is easy to get frustrated about conflicting reviews, the aim of review is to encourage enhancement, accuracy and scholarship. As reviewers have different expertise, different backgrounds, have read in different areas and specialise in different

2 Recommended reading is Professor Barbara Kamler's chapter (2010) about the role of 'publication brokers' when one goes to resubmit journal articles based on previous reviews.

fields, they are unlikely to come up with the same points that need to be improved or reworked. They are going to give the best feedback they can, based on what they know and how they have learnt what it is they know.

Establishing the paradigm or theoretical frameworks used can be a difficult process, so some further reading about paradigms, the 'why of research' and methodology is recommended. There are various, multiple texts available. In a paper given at a postgraduate research weekend in 1998 (at Central Queensland University, Australia), Professor Trevor Gale (1998) claimed that one of the reasons researchers can be very enthusiastic in support of their own research and its position is because it is so directly related to who they are as individuals. The researcher you are is the person you are – hence why negative reviews are often taken so personally! You have to distance yourself from your research so you are not cut up every time someone thinks differently to you, that is, that your work has 'holes' or 'issues'.



Yet, you should not take the disappointments and rejections personally. While some unfortunate occurrences can be linked to personal rivalry or vendettas, the rejections or requests for resubmissions are almost always about academia's overall commitment to the quality and distribution of valid and esteemed knowledge and research. You need to remember that 'the production of knowledge by academics is an inherently sociopolitical and cultural activity' (Kenway, Gough and Hughes 1998: 9).

Learn how to succeed in the jungle. Learn the climate. Learn about the pitfalls. Learn what is against you and for you. Learn how to hack a path. Learn which path is the right one for you. Do not just take only one path. The final destination (in this case, journal publications) needs to be carefully navigated. It is not an easy task to have an article published, but each time it happens, it is immensely satisfying – it is the sign of successful negotiation of a crowded jungle.

You may get stuck in the mud. You may have to nurse your insect bites. You may have to take time out from hacking one path in favour of another. You do need to develop thick skin to protect yourself from the sun (burn), the mosquitoes and the cold nights. But as much as you do to prepare for your journey, there are always unknowns – things that take you by surprise, pathways that disappoint or terrain that leads you nowhere. All of these challenges will make you stronger and a better scholar. Relish the challenge!

# 6 Stamina is Needed for Survival: Choosing the Right Journal

This chapter highlights the various items crucial to the successful submission of an article to a journal. The extensive list of conventions for each particular journal is of utmost importance to consider. While writing for one particular journal in mind is great when you start a fresh research project, changing the audience that a PhD thesis was intended for and finding a new path or avenue for publishing part of your thesis is taxing.

Details are given in this chapter about how to choose the 'right' or most suitable journal for your research to be published. A journal profiling checklist is provided so you can précis the preferences or biases of each journal to determine the appropriateness for your work. These are guidelines, but they are not guarantees. By doing your research about the suitability of a journal for the publication of your research, you are increasing your stamina, that is, your chances of success. While it may take longer to profile the journals and 'do your homework', this means that you are being clever about which avenues you utilise to submit your work for publication. Your increased stamina and the chances of success over a period of time will be well worth it.

While it may have been advantageous to provide you with a database of journals, their conventions and their history, it is unmistakable that this is a job only you can do; it is part of learning to 'play the game' or 'navigate the jungle'. The various breadth of specialities that we as academics have mean that a database that suits your particular needs would not only be difficult to produce, but it would be difficult to provide another one for the next person from a different field with a different epistemological position. Because only you know where your paradigm lies according to the lay of the land, only you can decide which journals have an appropriate 'fit' with you and your work.

This chapter will also give an example of a cover letter, which is possibly overlooked nowadays, due to the fact that we tend to either email our manuscripts to an editorial assistant, or we submit online via a Manuscript System. Sometimes cover letters are not required, but in many cases they are needed so you can state that the manuscript is original, not published elsewhere, alongside a declaration about how you believe the article fits within the aims and scope of the journal.

## ALL ALONE IN THE THICK BUSH

In reading the literature surrounding the 'how to' of publishing, it remains of crucial significance that the most effort surrounding writing an article should actually go into the research and selection of a journal to which your article 'fits'. While you can labour long and hard in writing, crafting and editing your article, it will be of no use to you should you mistakenly select a journal not sympathetic to your theoretical, conceptual or methodological approach. The process of choosing the right journal and then crafting your article for submission to that journal takes many, many hours. A whole raft of things must be considered, which are detailed in the publications mentioned in Chapter 1. A mammoth effort is needed to 'get it right'.



The title of this chapter, 'Stamina is needed for survival', is apt. It takes a careful, conscientious, particular and painstaking amount of effort to submit a journal article. If you do not put in this effort, your chances of rejection increase exponentially. Many journal articles do not go out for review because they do not suit the purposes and aims of the journal, nor the readership of the journal. Many journal articles lack clarity in their intent and confuse the reader. Writing a journal article is not about creating your utopian article that advocates your idealistic notions of the research you have conducted, existing only in an innocuous vacuum of ingenuity. The guidelines and IFA must be adhered to.

> *Personal creativity is discouraged. Journals exist to disseminate knowledge to a learned audience and are therefore obliged to set and maintain standards. Your personal preference for style or approach will not be as important as your ability to adhere to guidelines. (Black et al. 1998: 42)*

The process of ensuring your article 'fits' in form and content with the journal takes a long time. If you have not appropriately researched which journal is appropriate for your work, you will have wasted all the time trying to 'fit' with the stylistic conventions of the journal you chose.

If and when you find out that you have submitted an article to the wrong journal, it is because you did not take the required time needed to ensure it was a good fit. That said, I was surprised once when an article I submitted to an American journal did not go out for review, because of this very reason. I thought I had gotten it right; I thought I had profiled it accurately. (I did not use the journal profiling checklist below though!)

I have a friend and colleague who submitted her PhD thesis in January 2009. The following week, her supervisor sat down with her and identified how she could carve up her thesis into suitable articles for two different journals. Before she even began compiling the articles, she had the journal and its audience in mind. Based on her supervisor's experience, she was able to make a quality decision of where she should submit her work. This is an ideal scenario, and I think she is very lucky to have a supervisor who had an idea of how she should establish her nascent career.



In researching the profile of the journal, you should ask the advice of those who have already published in the journal. What has been their experience? You should also ask yourself, what group of journals correspond with your interests? Kenway, Gough and Hughes ask, 'Are the authors of these debates the people whose work you know and are they the people you would like to know your work?' (1998: 22). Are you familiar with the work of those that sit on the editorial board? If you want to be positioned amongst those scholars, then that journal is possibly appropriate for you. Questions to ask yourself about a potential journal include:

- Does the journal value the type of research you did?
- Has the journal published similar topics to yours?
- What types of research or focus does the editorial board have?

As they value what they do, if your work is similar along the themes of the questions above, they will tend to value yours also. For instance, while I have admired the authors published in the *British Journal of Sociology of Education*, I have concluded that my PhD study was not 'big' enough, nor was my theoretical engagement 'big' enough to warrant publication in that journal. Having said that, their policy is not to continually revise and review ongoing submissions. Two strikes and you are out. This is a prestigious journal in which I aim (one day) to have my work published, so when I have a 'big project' I will have to shape a subsequent article into one that suits the readership of the journal, the theoretical nature of the journal and the conventions of that journal.

## JOURNAL PROFILING

Craswell (2005) details the various conventions you should research in building a journal profile. He emphasises the importance of studying the style and structure of articles previously published in the journal. This includes linguistic features, organisational features and treatment of information (Craswell 2005). I have been influenced by much of what he has suggested in developing the following checklist for building a journal profile. As was the case with the checklists in Chapter 1, the following journal profiling checklist (Table 6.1) was also reviewed by most of the academics featured in this book.

**Table 6.1 Journal profiling checklist**

| | **Item** | **Description** |
|---|---|---|
| 1 | Title | |
| 2 | Readership (audience) | |
| 3 | Purposes (scope and aims) | |
| 4 | Impact factor | |
| 5 | Journal ranking | |
| 6 | Ideological/paradigmatic preferences | |
| 7 | Methodological frameworks previously published | |
| 8 | Theoretical frameworks previously published | |
| 9 | Editorial board | |
| 10 | Indexed in which databases? | |
| 11 | How 'theory' is presented | |
| 12 | Typical headings and subheadings | |
| 13 | Website | |
| 14 | Does it publish philosophical/ theoretical articles, review articles, research notes, opinion pieces or empirical studies? | |
| 15 | Acceptance rate | |
| 16 | Turnaround time | |
| *17* | *Number of issues per year* | |
| *18* | *Number of articles in each issue* | |
| *19* | *Style of writing* | |
| *20* | *Length of articles* | |

*Source*: Influenced by Cantor (1993), Craswell (2005), Day (1996), Epstein, Kenway and Boden (2005), Kenway, Gough and Hughes (1998), and Wager, Godlee and Jefferson (2002).

The items in italics were questioned by one professor, but deemed important by another. The rationale for including each of these items will now be detailed as, while they may not be particularly applicable to your field, they may provide you with insightful and beneficial information.

### Number 1 Title

The title is usually a helpful descriptor of the journal's focus. However, the journal is usually categorised by keywords, which are also helpful and informative.

### Number 2 Readership and Number 3 Purposes

The 'information for authors' (IFA) will usually state who the journal's readership is marketed to, and the journal's scope (breadth) and aims (focuses). You need to clarify and confirm whether your work fits into these categories.



### Number 4 Impact factor

A prestigious journal is typically marked with a high impact factor (IF). Impact factors measure citations and therefore claim to be influential. They are calculated each year by Thomson Institute for Scientific Information and are published in what is known as Journal Citation Reports (JCR). Every year, the previous year's impact factors are calculated and published, for instance, the impact factors of 2010 are published during the northern hemisphere summer of 2011. An impact factor is 'a measure of the frequency with which the "average article" in a journal has been cited in a given period of time' (Science Gateway 2009). The impact factor for a journal is calculated based on a three-year period, and can be considered to be the average number of times published papers are cited up to two years after publication. For example, the impact factor 2009 for a journal would be calculated as follows:

> *A = the number of times articles published in 2008–9 were cited in indexed journals during 2010*
>
> *B = the number of articles, reviews, proceedings or notes published in 2008–9*
>
> *impact factor 2010 = A/B (Science Gateway 2009).*

What we can glean from this is that citations are important. If you are able to demonstrate that someone has been citing your work, you can argue for a degree of influence or impact on the field, and claim to a certain extent, an international profile. Of course, citations can be positive or negative, but what is recorded is the amount of times your journal articles are mentioned in other articles. Books are not indexed in the way journal articles are, so they do not receive impact factors. Perhaps that is why journal articles have arguably more kudos in some ways. They become part of the academic discourse more readily as they can be indexed, measured and evaluated. Science Gateway (2010) lists the high impact journals in every field, while in-cites (2008) lists the top education and educational research journals (as they were in 2006).

While journals with impact factors (some are available on the journal's home page, while others are increasingly difficult to discover) above 1.0 are considered 'prestigious' (I have chosen this number because a: there are not many journals over the impact factor of 1.0, and b: most journals have an impact factor, if at all, of 0.1–0.9), they probably have a higher rejection rate because they are esteemed. Therefore, in order to keep their respected position in that field, they can afford to only print those articles that are outstanding. They do not care if they reject nine out of ten journal articles, because they *do not need* to print your work. They *need* to print outstanding research. And that is what they will do. It is in their best interests. Hence, I suggest if you are a nascent researcher that it may be worth your while to establish yourself with publication in less prestigious journals, and build up your research and extend your PhD to become more comprehensive, and then submit to and aim for the more prestigious journals. This is my opinion and is what I, am working towards. Professor Sara Dolnicar, who features in Chapter 15, strongly suggests taking a portfolio approach, whereby not only do you submit articles to the top journals, but you also submit work to B and C journals so that you compile a portfolio. She warns against putting all eggs in one basket because there is no guarantee that work will be successful in publication (or winning research grants) despite the amount of effort that is put into a project. It may just 'kill your career' if you only seek out high-quality outlets, because while you are waiting three years for your journal article to be accepted, a lot of your career is passing you by – you are missing out on other opportunities to develop your profile, whether it may be through publishing in professional publications or B and C journals. Some top journals are merciless in their reviews, and these may not be particularly helpful to you in the burgeoning stage of your career. This is not to say that you should give up on your goals or only publish in mediocre outlets, but you do need to be realistic about which paths you can successfully hack through the jungle.

## Number 5 Journal ranking

As part of the Australian Research Council (ARC), the Excellence in Research Australia (ERA) initiative has provided rankings of journals respective to their fields.[1] 'A-star' journals are top. These rankings provide another reference point in addition to impact factor. If you can claim that you have published in A-star or A journals, then your work will be considered to be of better quality than if it is published in C journals or if it is published in unranked journals. At the time of writing (January 2010), only two of the ten clusters had been drafted and revised (see Lamp 2010). The Field of Research (FoR) Codes, as defined by the Australian Bureau of Statistics, are used to help identify and rank the journals according to four tiers. This is one example of how Australia is using a system to determine quality. (The full list of FoR codes (categories) can be found at ARC (2009a).)

The following, interesting and particularly pertinent information was accessed from ARC (2009c):



> A* [A-star]
>
> *Typically an A* journal would be one of the best in its field or subfield in which to publish and would typically cover the entire field/subfield. Virtually all papers they publish will be of a very high quality. These are journals where most of the work is important (it will really shape the field) and where researchers boast about getting accepted. Acceptance rates would typically be low and the editorial board would be dominated by field leaders, including many from top institutions.*
>
> A
>
> *The majority of papers in a Tier A journal will be of very high quality. Publishing in an A journal would enhance the author's standing, showing they have real engagement with the global research community and that they have something to say about problems of some significance. Typical signs of an A journal are lowish acceptance rates and an editorial board which includes a reasonable fraction of well known researchers from top institutions.*
>
> B
>
> *Tier B covers journals with a solid, though not outstanding, reputation. Generally, in a Tier B journal, one would expect only a few papers of*

1 During the writing of this book, the draft rankings of the Excellence in Research (ERA) Australia rankings were drawn upon. After I submitted the manuscript to the publisher, the 'final lists of the current rankings' were released and are available at Lamp (2010) and ARC (2009b). However, these rankings are in many ways very different from the draft rankings. According to some (author included), they are in many respects disputable.

*very high quality. They are often important outlets for the work of PhD students and early career researchers. Typical examples would be regional journals with high acceptance rates, and editorial boards that have few leading researchers from top international institutions.*

C

*Tier C includes quality, peer reviewed, journals that do not meet the criteria of the higher tiers.*

This is quite possibly a draft that will continue to be refined, but it is worth considering when you are profiling particular journals. In 2008–2009, the ARC received submissions about opinions surrounding which journals were deemed to be in which tier.



Previously, the 'Research Quality Framework' was in existence by the former Australian federal government. In 2008, the United Kingdom used a framework entitled the 'Research Assessment Exercise' (HEFCE 2009). Changing governments and expectations require that academics are savvy and up to date with requirements and understandings about what is considered to be 'valuable'. You need to find out how 'quality' and 'output' are measured and determined by your country, as tenure, promotion, funding and status are dependent on this.

## Numbers 6, 7 and 8 Conflicting paths

When I refer to epistemology and ontology, I am referring to the theories that we believe to be true about knowledge and about reality. For example, the epistemology of feminism is explained to be:

> *What this means, in practice, is that the lens through which we view the world is shaped by certain understandings about gender, power and the position of women. So an epistemology may be defined as a particular sort of lens that allows you to make sense of some aspect of the world around you in a particular way. Different lenses (different epistemologies) will obviously give different views. No epistemology can give you a total view of the world, because they only allow you to see from particular perspectives. (Boden, Kenway and Epstein 2005: 41)*

Your personal philosophy, or worldview (the way you see the world), which encompasses epistemology (the nature of knowledge) and ontology (the nature of reality) informs and shapes how you go about your everyday life, your research and your writing. Being aware of what worldview you actually do have, and what allegiances the editorial board of the journal align themselves with, is crucial to determine. Again, this is not an easy task, but it is something you can get better at doing. Sometimes, academics will write for the journal in mind and 'sell their soul' in a way, in order to get an article published in a prestigious journal. They will utilise methodologies or theories that the journal values, but not ones the author values, in order to obtain a publication. This is another way to navigate the jungle.

## Number 9 Editorial board

If you know of the people on the editorial board, if you have read their work, and if you tend to read the articles published in that journal, then it is possible this journal might be the best avenue to submit your work. What kind of research do these editorial board members do? If you do not know of the editorial board members at all, this should not dissuade you, however, you need to be able to justify to yourself why you should spend the time writing an article for that particular journal. If you have a conflicting ideology to the editor, it is possible your work will not be considered for publication in that journal because that is not what is currently valued. That is their right as an editor. Persons who are professional may seek to publish a complementary array of perspectives, but if the article has a limited aim or scope, or if it is contrary to the aims and scope of the journal, then again, they do not *need* to publish your work, which will stick out like a sore thumb.



## Number 10 Indexing

If the journal lists the databases in which its articles are indexed, then that increases the chances that potential readers might come across your work, that is, through Internet search engines. If a journal does not have its articles indexed in databases, then this possibly decreases the distribution of your work. Database inclusion is likely to increase the possibility of people citing your work, and therefore increase the impact factor of the journal in which you are published. This is a factor to consider, but for early career researchers, it is perhaps not a top priority. For some academics, where a journal is indexed is not a concern because they receive alerts about recently published journal issues and methodically read their favoured journal content anyway. The journal *Children's Literature in Education* lists the following on its home page that details where the journal is abstracted and indexed:

> *Abstracted/Indexed in: Academic OneFile, Academic Search, Arts & Humanities Citation Index, Current Abstracts, Current Contents/Arts and Humanities, Education Research Index, Educational Research Abstracts Online (ERA), ERIC System Database, Gale, Google Scholar,*

*Humanities International Index, HW Wilson, MathEDUC, MLA International Bibliography, OCLC, SCOPUS, Sociology of Education Abstracts, Summon by Serial Solutions, TOC Premier. (Springer 2010)*

## Number 11 How 'theory' is presented

See Chapter 5. What you understand 'theory' to be and what makes sense to you will be reflected in which journals you like or 'click with' because your view of the world will also be demonstrated in the way that authors within particular journals also understand theory. This item is closely aligned with items 6, 7 and 8.

## Number 12 Typical headings and subheadings

While some items on the checklist may not be particularly helpful or relevant for your field of work, other items such as 'typical headings and subheadings' will actually indicate to you the 'ideological/paradigmatic preferences'. Some journals are very particular about how they want each article structured. For instance, classic headings such as 'background', 'literature review' and 'methods' might be compulsory. Other journals prefer descriptive, non-traditional subheadings. The IFA or 'guidelines for submission' may explain these conventions.



## Number 13 Website

Very helpful information can be found on a journal's website, such as the IFA. Some of the information for the items in the journal profiling checklist will be able to be found in the journal's IFA. Bookmarking the Internet websites of your favoured journals in a particular folder on your web browser is a good idea.

## Number 14 Types of publications

Some journals do not publish empirical research, but focus more on commentary and 'big picture stuff'. Other journals will only publish empirical research; others focus only on methodology. Three types of articles that are published were mentioned in Chapter 3 and detailed in Chapter 5. It is important that you assess what articles are mostly printed in the journal in which you are profiling. This will help you to establish whether the likelihood of your theoretical essay-type article has a chance of publication.

## Numbers 15 and 16 Acceptance rate and Turnaround time

The information for some items, such as #15 and #16, may not be public. As indicated in Chapter 4, some editorial boards do not disclose the acceptance rates for their journal. You may have to consult other people who have published in that journal to find out the turnaround time. If you know the acceptance rate for a particular journal, you might never submit to it if the rate is very low. Sometimes it is better not to know – it may put you off from attempting to carve that pathway.

Another aspect that is becoming a concern for many academics is the time from acceptance of an article to the actual publication of the article. Many journals are now publishing their accepted articles online so others can access them before the actual hard copy of the printed issue is published. However, if what counts is 'lines on your CV', then you may make a decision to publish in a journal with a quick turnaround rather than one where you will be waiting for your article to be published in two to three years time.



## Numbers 17 and 18 Number of issues and Number of articles

The number of issues per year may increase the possible impact factor. However, this is dependent on the amount of submissions. In recent times, those journals that have been ranked highly have often received more submissions than usual because of the pressure upon academics to be published in journals with esteem. If a journal only publishes two issues a year, with only four articles per issue, the places for publication are limited. It seems logical to state that if a journal is published twice a year and only has four articles per issue, then anyone's chance of publication in that journal is low. If you choose a journal that publishes eight issues a year and has eight articles in each issue, then your chances of publication are increased because there are more available places. However, all of this depends on the amount of (quality) submissions received. Knowing this kind of information might enable you to avoid a long delay between acceptance and being in print. However, this is not a given. What may be more of a concern to you is whether you think the journal is a good one, and whether you want to be published within it. One of the academics featured in this book shared an anecdote where a student of theirs had boasted about a recent journal publication, but as the academic did not think highly of the journal, they thought the publication was probably more of a hindrance than a benefit. What is published is more or less permanent and cannot be erased. Some things take a long time to be forgotten.

### Number 19 Style of writing

This is covered in more detail in the checklists on 'form' and 'content' in Chapter 1.

### Number 20 Length of articles

This may seem to be an obvious point or an irrelevant one, but the fact remains that if journals only publish articles from 3,000–4,000 words, then your draft of 8,000 words will not be suitable. If you have a 10,000-word chapter, it is unlikely that you will be able to cull it down to a 5,000-word version successfully (see Chapter 9). Submitting an article for review that is over the 7,000-word maximum means that you are giving the reviewers another reason to reject your work.



## IS IT WORTH THE EFFORT?

You may be thinking that this checklist seems onerous. You may be thinking that there is not enough time in the day to do this research. However, when someone says to you, 'do your research' or 'do your homework', this is an example of what they mean. Profiling each journal is essential to increase your chances of success of submitting to a journal likely to accept your work for publication. I have a close friendship with a fellow early career researcher who was interested in this manuscript. Michelle and I have discussed on many occasions the challenges and issues associated with 'starting out' in an academic career. She raised questions about rejection and suitable avenues for publication. So prior to sending this manuscript to the publisher, I gave her the journal profiling checklist (and this draft chapter). What follows is her contribution about the process of profiling a number of journals according to the checklist.

### The Journal Profiling Checklist – A Documented Experience

As an early career researcher, the journal profiling checklist was suggested as a way of understanding and cataloguing the journals that might be relevant to current research projects. With a list of journals searched out on the ERA list and copies of the journal profiling checklist in hand, the detailed job of creating a profiling checklist of each journal began.

For the most part when utilising the checklist, online research revealed the basic information about the journal in question such as the number of copies produced, purposes of the journal, readership and the submission guidelines (for example, style of writing, length of articles and the editorial board). A basic search engine provided information regarding the website address of the journal or where it could be accessed online as well.

However, pathways to the more detailed criteria in regards to academic submission such as ideological preferences, methodological frameworks and theoretical frameworks and the specific types of articles accepted were more difficult to obtain via online searches. This information was found by taking the time to peruse some of the volumes of the journal and/or some published articles within, to review, summarise and catalogue in order to make inferences or gather reliable data about these particular criteria as outlined on the checklist.

Furthermore, some specific criteria such as acceptance rates and turnaround times were also unlikely to be located via online searches. This information was not readily available when reviewing submission guidelines.



Gathering data regarding the impact factor and journal ranking of each journal proved to be one of the most time consuming tasks. Using links to the published Journal Citation Reports (JCR) provided details for only a few of the selected journals, based on the JCR system used in ranking journals. Downloading a copy of rankings from the ARC (www.arc.gov.au) website also proved useful, however, again this was a time consuming task where a full list was needed to be viewed and then funnelled down to the specific journals that were desired.

Another resource that was used in this process was that of the academic research librarian at the local university library. Her expertise and knowledge of the search engines and academic rankings was a great aid to this exercise.

Although this process was very time consuming and at times painstakingly slow, the end product is a concise, well defined, organised catalogue of the journals that will prove to be valuable for the submission of research specific academic work. These completed criteria lists will be used as a guideline and reference for future academic articles for years to come (supplied by Michelle Eady and Keira-Lee Metcalfe, January 2010).

## KEEP YOUR BEARINGS

If you are new to the realm of academia, in that you are hoping to publish from research conducted in your postgraduate study, or you are a practitioner in the profession rather than an academic, you may find this rather overwhelming. That is why I call it a jungle. It is overwhelming because it is unfamiliar, it is unknown and it is vast. Realising this may help you to fathom the amazing success of those who have successfully navigated their jungle. Having the suggestion made that you should publish your work is a compliment, but getting the work published is a difficult journey. That said, it is arguable that success is measured by what you give up in order to achieve. There is a price to pay for any type of achievement. If it were easy to publish, everyone would do it. There would be no need for this book or the many others that detail the 'how to' of academic writing.

## THE COST OF THE JOURNEY

There are various prices to pay when undertaking a PhD that you have to weigh up as to their worth and whether the sacrifice of them is worth it in the long run. Fewer social engagements, fewer friends, less leisure and recreation time, less sleep and little money are a few of the costs to pay. A colleague of mine, Dr Gordon Brown, told me of an article he had read about 'what not to do during your PhD'. It included move house, get married, have a child, change job and so on, because of the fact that doing a PhD requires so much effort and focus that too many other stressors will make your effort and focus impotent. A tertiary educator of mine, Dr Bob Katterns, once told me that doing a PhD was a young person's vocation because of the energy, drive and ruthlessness of focusing only on the PhD. While this book is not about writing and finishing a PhD, what I wish to highlight is that if you have made the sacrifice required to submit and have your doctorate conferred, then you are also capable of having your work published. The process of writing an article for journal review also requires much effort and focus. However, it requires more energy, a different focus and an understanding of the 'new jungle'. Brabazon (2009b) captured it well when she stated:

> *At the point of submitting a PhD, we all think nothing will ever be as difficult. Only later do we realise that the PhD was a singular, special opportunity to concentrate on a project and topic in a supportive environment, enabled by people who cared about our research. The PhD is an apprenticeship. The career commences after the examination.*
>
> *The unfortunate truth is that completing a PhD is easier than building a career.*

Writing an assignment or thesis and writing for a journal is like chalk and cheese. Therefore, realise the processes involved, realise the role of the intellectual gatekeepers, and revitalise yourself enough so you can focus on the new task at hand – publication in journals.

Another option before you submit your article for review is to send a screen email to the editor to see if she or he seems interested in your abstract. When I asked journal editors for numbers regarding their acceptance rates of the previous calendar year, many responded quickly. This was encouraging. So while your journal article may take a long time to be reviewed and rebuffed or accepted, sending a screen email about your possible abstract and consequent article may increase the speed of eventual publication (and a successfully navigated path). That said, many editors would prefer you put in the work needed to craft and hone your article so that it suits their journal. On the other hand, many editors did not reply to my email request.

## A GOOD COVER



Wager, Godlee and Jefferson (2002) explicitly state how to write a good cover letter. An example of a cover letter is included overleaf. It is important that your letter is free from spelling errors, especially that of the editor's and journal's name. A brief description of your findings and why the journal's readership would be interested in your work should be included. If possible, a reason for why your work should be published should be given, as well as an explanation of why you have chosen that journal as a receptacle for your work. You should also clarify that the article has not been submitted elsewhere and is an original work. It only takes a small amount of time to construct an appropriate cover letter, and while not all journal article submissions require a cover letter, it can give a good first impression of you if it is thoughtfully worded.

**Example Cover Letter**

*Dr Nicola F. Johnson*
*Faculty of Education*
*Monash University*
*Australia*

*The Editors (J. Bloggs, S. Brown)*
*The Very Interesting Journal*
*The Publisher*
*The Country*

*February 6, 2010*

*To whom it may concern:*

*Please find attached an original manuscript, not published before, that I am submitting for review to The Very Interesting Journal.*

*This article carefully explains the delivery of a subject I taught to pre-service teachers in 2009 and pedagogically analyses the blended learning approach. I think it will be of interest to readers of The Very Interesting Journal as it details how technology was integrated into the subject and how it went about increasing students' pedagogical and technical literacy.*

*I look forward to your reply.*

*Yours faithfully,*

*Nicola Johnson*

Cantor (1993) also gives examples of cover letters and requests for permission surrounding issues of copyright.

## THE FINAL SIGNPOST

As I have pointed out, it is imperative to consider the nature of the journal to which you are submitting an article. The way the journal's editorial board views the world has to be sympathetic to yours in order for your work to be published. That said, generally, a PhD is a relatively small study, so some journals only wish to publish significant work from established academics.

Despite the blind reviewing process, the reviewers may be able to ascertain that your work is small and that it originates from a beginning scholar. However, many journals want to provide opportunity for publishing, despite a 'newbie's' appeared lack of experience. Targeting the right journal requires a significant amount of research, reading, sifting and sorting. It demands that informed judgements be made. It involves a frank assessment of a journal's partiality and its favouritism. You will not be able to change its worldview. The likelihood of the journal publishing an article that does not meet its readership or aims or scope or conventions is nil. The journals that go out of their way to publish 'counter-intuitive perspectives' (Black et al. 1998: 43) are few. That said, you should not limit yourself; there may be an opportunity for you to submit work that develops a whole new discourse or continues a debate surrounding a new methodology or theoretical framework for instance. Questions to ask are whether you are brave enough, and can you spare the time to rigorously craft your work so that it fits that particular journal's demands?

## CONTINUING THE DEBATE: AN ALTERNATIVE STRATEGY

I am not saying that you should only publish in avenues where everyone else agrees with you. There is a place for debating the 'fors' and 'againsts' of any theoretical perspective or particular methodology. This is one way that intellect and arguments are honed. You should look to challenge ingrained (mis)beliefs, of course. You should be seeking to critique things you do not agree with. But the fact remains that the way people conduct research reflects the way they view knowledge and its quality. It is unlikely that qualitative research of a theoretical nature will ever get published in a journal that publishes only quantitative research.

In commenting on the journal profiling checklist, Professor Lori Lockyer (who features in Chapter 12) suggested that a helpful means for navigating the jungle is to continue a debate already appearing in a journal and present additional or differing findings in a way that demonstrates you have engaged with the previous research published in the journal and that you are enhancing and/or developing the debate surrounding the topic, research questions and so on. This may be of particular interest to an editorial board and the readership of the journal, especially if they have found it so interesting before that they have previously published work surrounding the topic. In either the cover letter and/or the introduction, it is important you state how you are extending the argument, because journals do not wish to publish work that repeats previously published articles and that does not contribute anything new. It is also imperative you make reference to articles previously published in that journal so that you show that you have engaged with the material and are subsequently familiar with the journal, its content, and its aims and scope. Both Lori Lockyer and Sara Dolnicar suggested that if there are specific people you have cited in your own work, look at where they have published, and that may help you to identify a suitable journal for your work.

The difficulty of establishing which journal is the right one for you to target is noted. Negotiating the crowded jungle is a complex journey that, upon commencement, you can only get better at navigating if you persist.

# 7 Fighting the Heat, Hunger and Thirst: Dealing with Rejection

Rejection happens, but few talk about it. There is quite a lot to learn about playing the academic game and developing a thick skin. This chapter suggests what you should do instead of deciding to give up, retreating into your shell or choosing another career.

You may not have similar feelings to me. I have taken the spears of rejection to heart and this has been damaging to my wellbeing and subjectivity. Rejection can be cruel. Earth-shattering in fact. The depths of despair always want residents. To be released from their clutches, much strength is required. Someone else can often offer you their hand to help, but ultimately you are the only one who can help yourself.

When I consider the wonderful people/academics I know who have received poignant rejections, I know that, without a doubt, rejection happens or has happened to everyone. A researcher's passion, vitality and skill cannot be captured in a journal article, nor should it, because the article should be assessed on its merit and the quality of the writing, not on the quality of the person who wrote it. A reviewer has to assess for the journal according to a set of criteria, or according to their understanding of how articles should be written. They are assessing the research, not the person. You might pronounce a reviewer to be biased, but it is possible to argue that every single one of us is biased. We each have an opinion as to what counts as 'good' research and 'good' writing. When you receive a rejection in academia, this needs to be framed as an opportunity to learn and grow. Resubmissions requested should be viewed as good news. Acceptances should be viewed as cause for celebration.

Rejections and acceptances are made according to beliefs. These beliefs are subjective, particular to that person, but usually this person – whoever it is

– has been educated by others about research and about writing. The journal's editorial board values them as a reviewer. That does not mean you will get similarly-minded reviews or reviewers! So, while a journal needs to protect its conventions and esteem, you can be assured that a rejection is not a definitive mark of a person's worth, nor of their ideas.

If you can position yourself to think that rejection is inevitable, then you are better off. Rather than expecting success, Luey advises to be prepared for criticism – perhaps we should be expecting it. She advises that, 'If you just want a pat on the back or uncritical encouragement, read the article to your dog' (Luey 2002: 15). There are benefits in receiving criticism and negative reviews. The intellectual gatekeepers can be of benefit to you as referees can save you from embarrassment in a number of forms. Your poor argument or neglect of literature or basic writing skills can be noted and improved. It is unlikely that your weak research will get published, although perhaps it will be published in a low-quality journal. The gatekeepers are ensuring that your ill-constructed ideas are challenged. It is hard to consider this as being positive, but it is.



If you receive a rejection, the gatekeeping and sifting is working. Your work will only be published in the appropriate places because the sifting that takes place only vetoes unsuitable articles. Those who submit low-quality work increase their chances of rejection, but those who submit their work to inappropriate venues are also asking to be rejected. Luey advises that you should always have a back-up plan, a second journal in mind to which you can submit your article should it be *returned*. She suggests the use of the word *returned* rather than *rejected*.

## THIS IS MY CAMP; YOU STAY IN YOURS

It is evident to me that, in the interests of self-preservation and self-importance, certain academics cannot support, nor do they try to understand or accept research that is different to theirs. Given the examples of high rejection rates in Chapter 4 and the methodological blindness and (unspoken) bias evident in academia, it is no wonder that rejection rates have high percentages. It is normal (but perhaps not for those who have learnt to navigate the jungle successfully).

Certain worldviews blind people from understanding other perspectives, including the refutation of methodology that in the certain person's eyes does not count as rigorous. This means that those who are closed-minded to new ideas, or different methods, not only limit themselves and their intellect by not being open to it, but they also place themselves in their own cocoon or bubble, where they surround themselves only with others whose interests are similar. This perpetuates the notion that their way is the best way and the only way.

So what does this mean? It means that some people will not 'get it'. They will not 'get' what you are doing and why you are doing it, because their worldview, whether pragmatic, positivist or critical means that they find it difficult to appreciate something they do not agree with or are not familiar with.

In the little experience I have had as an academic, I have been wedged between those that I deem to be practical researchers and those that I deem to be abstract researchers (please forgive the binary), all of whom I have found to be great at what they do, but sometimes unable to understand or appreciate the research or activity that goes on at the other end of the continuum. It has made for an uncomfortable position at times, because it seems I am able to acknowledge the vast array of what counts to be good educational research and cultural studies research. I am able to appreciate the various, differing intricacies of what that means, though the type of research in which I engage is obviously my preferred approach to research. Crossing the divide is not an easy journey.

Self-preservation counts. It is important. It is what ensures success. Having others validate your position is nice but, as an academic, your perspective must be secure in order to survive the rejections of those who disagree with your worldview.

The meaning of theory is another obstacle I have encountered. This word 'theory' means different things to different people. I am still trying to work it out. For example, in my PhD, I had a small sample of participants and conducted qualitative research in the vein similar to a case study approach, however, I engaged in depth with Pierre Bourdieu's sociological theories (habitus, capital, field, doxa, and so on). I used the theory to analyse my data and I generated themes from my data based on the theory. So my contribution to knowledge utilised a theory that was embedded right throughout the thesis. For some people, this would not count as a satisfactory PhD research project. They would dismiss this as being insufficient in terms of design and implementation. They would question the worth of the qualitative analysis based on such a small sample (n = 8).

However, I am coming to realise that because I engaged in the abstract critical theory to a deep level, that that is where the depth and weight of my PhD and therefore its rigour lies. For others, having a large sample and plenty of 'hard' data (figures, large sample, statistics, and so on) means they can present their data within their thesis without having to engage in complex sociological (abstract or critical) theories. For some of those based in educational psychology, for instance, their contribution to knowledge lies in the statistically significant generalisations able to be made from their data set, which proves or disproves their hypothesis. For some pragmatists in educational research, their contribution is made towards enhancing and further developing theories of learning.

However, a PhD is meant to make an original contribution to knowledge. If a thesis does not contribute to the theory of knowledge in some way, you have to question whether a PhD has in fact been completed. In the same way that someone may look down on a PhD candidate who performs a dance for his/her assessment, those who are positioned in contrasting methodological camps do not bother trying to meet up with you in the middle.

Therefore, the fact remains that if you submit an article to a journal that is not of the same 'bent' as you, it will be rejected. The methodological fascists are not interested in advocating or supporting ideas that are ideologically opposed to theirs. And who can blame them? I now explain why.

## THERE IS NO WAY THROUGH

Your first rejection is always tough and usually quite memorable. It is important not to take it personally. It is important to remember that rejection is common and that your chances of being accepted range from 5–25 per cent. As others have written (Black et al. 1998; Cantor 1993; Day 2008; Wager, Godlee and Jefferson 2002), you should read the reviews and, especially if they are harsh, put them aside for a few days, sleep on it, and come back to them afresh. It is essential that you thoroughly check the concerns to see if you agree with them.

A review should be read and the resulting blazing fire of wrath should invoke serious written response that should not be sent. Vent your disagreement in words or audio record your tirade, but then the article, reviews and your response should be placed to the side for at least 48 hours. At that time the review should be re-read with fresh eyes and the initial fiery retort should be perused with a calm disposition. You should then carefully number the reviewer's points and decide if they are reasonable according to the journal's conventions (usually specified in the guidelines to authors). You also need to ask yourself whether you actually understand what the reviewers are saying to you. Articulate clearly what it is that they do not like or understand about your article.

Many journals only want to publish studies that have tested hypotheses through qualitative and/or quantitative means. Other journals (and their editorial boards) refute the idea that hypotheses should be tested, suggesting that only research questions should be answered and that a study that actually 'did' something should be approved. The third type of article is concerned with the theorising of a particular concept in a bid to advance understanding in a particular area. Post-positivists tend to view this type of article as imaginative writing and may see no value in this sort of 'academic waffle'. There is little flexibility in terms of what type of article journals publish. A journal has almost its own identity in terms of its paradigmatic, theoretical and methodological lens. In the same way that thesis examiners are carefully chosen due to their crucial role in ensuring a candidate's success, the success of an article's submission to a journal lies in the thorough selection of an appropriate journal for your work. Broadly speaking, a journal is ensuring its success by rejecting articles that are in non-agreement with the way it sees the world. It also claims high levels of prestige when it can boast a high rejection rate. Therefore, in a way, it seems that you should expect rejection from certain journals as it is in their best interests to do so, no matter how good your work is. You will not win a paradigm war.

Systematically, you must address each reviewer's point and write a response to it if you are going to resubmit it as a revision. The one great thing about rejections is that you can constantly improve your work by incorporating the feedback and then resubmitting it to another journal. The journal that accepts your article is the one that is methodologically and 'theoretically' (whatever that means) in agreement with you.

## HACK ANOTHER PATH

I may have used this subheading before, but now it is time to revise your article, polish it up again (and then again), and resubmit it to a more suitable choice of journal. Once, I received a rejection on a Saturday morning, was absolutely upset and angered, spent the day revising it according to the feedback and submitted it to another journal at 5pm. Needless to say, that journal also rejected the article. I had not spent enough time choosing the right journal for my work. The path I hacked was hopeless, it was hasty and I exerted unnecessary effort doing so. I needed to take a step back from the work and the negative review, and then try again, once I was refocused on a new and appropriate path.

## DON'T GIVE UP

I tend to have a habit of thinking the worst and inexplicably having a negative response to rejections. Personally, I have to work very hard on changing my negative thoughts to realistic ones in response to negative reviews or harsh rejections. In writing this book, I have realised that rejection is widespread and no statistician would disagree. So, accepting the fact that chances are swayed towards rejection, starts to put things into perspective. When selecting the top journals, it is a lofty goal, but it is only with 'similarly-minded' journals that you really have a chance. These 'similarly-minded' journals may not be the high-impact, top-quality journals you desire. But what we must remember is that any PhD thesis or dissertation is not the work equivalent of a Nobel Prize. While it is a significant contribution and a meaty project that we have slaved over, it may not be the type of substantial study (regardless of what methodology or theory you use) that the top journals tend to pick. For me, I know that I must build on the work I completed during my PhD candidature, and expand, and broaden, and deepen the quality and quantity of the work I accomplished. This is part of establishing my research profile as an early career academic. At the time of writing, it seems to me that I need to establish 'bigger' studies in order to make 'bigger' contributions that can then be published in 'bigger' journals.

Surviving peer review is difficult and can be a thoroughly draining process. For people like myself who are sensitive, analytical and reflective, the fear of not measuring up is a heavy burden. The slightest bit of doubt can develop into serious negativity. The work which has been produced by blood, sweat and tears is questioned when it is put up for review and, indeed, the reviews can create more tears. Your intellect, your nous, your epistemological position and your creativity are all unwillingly up for debate. You have to sincerely believe in the quality of these aspects and at times agree to disagree with the reviewers. Not everyone will agree with you, and not everyone will agree with each other, despite the best argument you may be able to put together. Rife are the dangers of personally succumbing to the rejection inherent in a written review. You must be sure of your epistemology and methodology in order to bear the brunt of personal or professional attacks (hopefully in the form of constructive criticism) on your work.

## THE FEAR OF THE UNKNOWN

When trying to carve a path through an unwelcome jungle, it is of no surprise that you may be quite afraid. I liken the submission of journal articles to being in an unknown, unwelcome environment. You do not know where you stand and you do not know how far you are progressing. The landmarks are slim. The weather intolerable and the pests ubiquitous. It can be very unpleasant. But it can be thrilling and pleasing when you get it right.

When I go to write, I tend to try and do everything else I can think of before I actually start typing. For instance, the dishwasher must be emptied, the dogs' water bucket filled up, the meat gotten out for dinner (from the freezer). All of my emails must be answered and I must not have any other pressing jobs. Is my desk tidy? Have I put out the rubbish? What else can I do to avoid writing? Then, and only then can I begin writing.[1] But I have to make myself write. Though I enjoy it and I get a buzz out of writing some point vividly and succinctly (which I find I have some difficulty doing verbally), it is an effort. It is a discipline. It is far easier to get involved in the administration of minor emails or pushing paper around or reading updates of others' blogs rather than getting to the business of writing.



That said, within the process of composing, drafting, revising, crafting and editing, I constantly travel through waves of feeling utterly incapable of doing what I have set out to do. As of 6 February 2009, I had had my first book released, had two journal articles from my PhD accepted for publication and just obtained the contract for this book, so at that time of writing, I should have been feeling pretty good about myself. But no, even now I waiver between being afraid of what others might think, and then at times feel totally overwhelmed by the magnitude of creating a sequential, well-argued manuscript that must be finely honed into a work of art. There is pressure to perform from academia, but I do also tend to put it on myself.

As we – via Abby Day – have discussed earlier (Chapter 1), there are substantial reasons for why we must publish. But there are also acceptable reasons for why we do not. The fear of failure, the fear of rejection, the fear of judgement. It is a constant and intimidating effort to write, submit and have a journal article accepted. It requires a thick skin. It is no wonder that some people with doctorates avoid the process! It also requires mental toughness, cerebral resilience and having belief that your work deserves to be published.

It is apparent I believe there is a need for candour. I may be erring on the side of being disarmingly honest here, but even as I was reading the draft proof of my first book, I thought to myself, 'Why would anyone want to read this?' Now I am pretty sure that book will not win any awards, but what I can say is that that book captured a period of my life where I truly believed in the argument I was making. I thoroughly read and synthesised

1 I acknowledge that this is a luxury, and quite possibly a result of chosen childlessness.

the literature surrounding the ideas in the book, and I made every effort I could to craft the book into a well-written publication. But, to be honest, I am scared that somebody might hate it. On the other hand, who cares? Someone undoubtedly will hate it! Someone will definitely disagree with the ideas and call me all sorts of names. This may be troublesome to me when it does happen and, again, the waves of self-doubt will wash over me, but what remains is that *I have written an actual book and I am a published author.* I did it. I put my ideas on paper. I fought against the self-doubt and the constant questioning of my ability to write. And what I can say now, is that I am happy with what I produced and I have to steel myself against what might be less than positive reviews.

## SELF-DOUBT IS NORMAL, JUST AS IS REJECTION



In a jungle the heat, the hunger and the thirst can be debilitating. A 'thick skin' is not enough. The blazing sun, the lack of food and the dehydration can really test your mettle. Survival is the name of the game. Opening yourself up to peer review and scrutiny is tough on your self-esteem, especially when the results are negative.

Another alarming fact is that many academics will not admit when their work has been rejected. It seems to me as though this is taboo. It appears as if admitting failure is admitting humanity. Others give the impression that to acknowledge negative judgement is to admit inferiority. We feel disdained if we are rejected. Our work is deemed 'not good enough'. However, as the anecdotes in this book demonstrate, rejections (as do mistakes) make us who we are and actually lead us on the road to success. If we do not accept our limitations, and the fact that we may just have submitted our work to the wrong journal, or perhaps we did not clearly argue our case for the significance of the article, then there is no pride in that. But if we truly believed we did our best work, submitted it (yay, well done, you are on the way!), and then are rejected, we can hold our heads proud. The subsequent/consequent revision and editing helps us to improve. It finely hones our work and who we are.

It is not a matter of 'if' your work will get rejected; it is a matter of 'when' your work will get rejected. You *will* get your work rejected. Some time, somewhere, some place by someone, your work will get rejected. It is just a matter of when, not if.

The other frustrating thing about all of this, is that while one person thinks your work is great it will be abhorrent to another. They will hate it. It is all to do with ideological positions and beliefs about what constitutes good writing. This is a subjective matter (Epstein, Kenway and Boden 2005).

## YOU DON'T DESERVE TO BE IN THE JUNGLE: YOU'RE NOT A 'REAL' ACADEMIC

It seems that in order for academics to have their place in the field validated, they must be negative and critical. When going about writing a review, if a reviewer is presented with an excellent manuscript, they may be tempted to pick invisible holes in the text simply because it would 'look bad' on them if they could not find something to be critical about.

> *We are educated to be critical and judgmental. To be supportive and positive is viewed as being weak. This is especially evident in academia. It is very difficult for academics to consider something and respond to it without feeling that they must come up with something negative to say. Women who are trying to gain acceptance into the academic world notice this and say, 'Even when we like something and think it is good, we know that our colleagues will not listen to us unless we find something wrong with it. We have to go out of our way to find something to criticize'. (Schaef 1987: 79)*



The (mis)conception is that you are not a 'real' academic, or a credible one until you can find something to criticise. Therefore, as an early career researcher, you should expect this type of critique from reviewers. They need to be negative to save face amongst their peers. The mindset is that they must be hole pickers of the nitty-gritty. So, you need to acknowledge this, as well as acknowledge that you have the right to disagree with the reviewers and state why.

## FOUR POSSIBLE PATHS

There are four possibilities that can occur when you submit an article. Your article can be rejected outright by the editor and not sent out for review. This will most likely be because your article does not suit the readership and purposes of the journal (or perhaps the methodological preference for large sample sets). The second possibility is that it will be rejected after review. As many publishing decisions are subjective (Cantor 1993), there are probably good reasons for this, including the plight that many authors subject themselves to, that of not researching the various facets that make up a journal. Your article will not be published by a journal that is not sympathetic to the ideology, epistemology, ontology, methodology and style of writing (form and content) to which you have adhered (Boden, Kenway and Epstein 2005). The third possibility is that you will be asked to revise your article and resubmit it based on the reviews of the referees. This is very positive and suggests that you have sent your article to the 'right' journal. However, this is not a guaranteed acceptance. That is the fourth possibility, which really is a cause for much celebration. It is a rarity to have an article accepted without revision or resubmission. Crack open the champagne! This last option is usually subject to editorial changes, which may be typos, of which you will have the chance to address when you are in the proofing stage.

When you are asked to resubmit an article after it has been reviewed by others, and revised by yourself as the author, you should have addressed all the points that the reviewers have made. Though you do not have to make all the changes the reviewers suggest, you do need to answer all of their concerns in a systematic way (Wager, Godlee and Jefferson 2002). On many occasions, the reviewers will give conflicting advice, which is frustrating, but that common phenomenon demonstrates the subjectivity of peer review. In the instance of having conflicting reviews, you have to decide which review you agree with the most, and then systematically discuss in your letter of reply to the editor why you have agreed with one reviewer and addressed their points, and then dismissed the other's review. Sometimes, it is a subjective view of what counts as 'real' research, and 'academic' writing, whether it be in the form of an ideological, methodological or stylistic point of difference that will be the conflicting issue. However, it may be an obvious and common occurrence, that of not clearly stating the focus and purpose of the paper. You may not have clarified the rationale for the study. You may not have provided appropriate detail for the methods you used. That said, it is important to place any review to the side for a few days, so you can consider it objectively and thoughtfully, without taking it personally.



Another frustrating expectation of authors is that they address the reviews quickly and not only resubmit the article according to the editor's deadlines and stipulations for acceptance, but also check the proofs in a very prompt manner. This is frustrating only because the reviews usually have taken a long time (over a year in many cases), but as Day (2008) points out, journal editors and reviewers are very busy people with a big job to do, and their level of frustration is notable, especially when authors like me send their work to their journal which is not a suitable venue for its publication.

When you submit a journal article for review, you are taking a risk. That is acknowledged. However, you can insulate yourself from the fallout of taking a risk that was unsuccessful by realising that this risk must be taken in order to achieve a desired result (whatever your goal is for publication). You should acknowledge that the process of submission, review, revision and publication is one of carving a path through a jungle that will only make the challenges of navigating the journey to the next destination an easier one. Taking the risk is worth it. It will not only make you tougher, it will refine your thinking. It will improve your writing. It will enhance your contribution to the academic discourse of your field.

## DOES THIS SOUND FAMILIAR?

I feel like a fake, you say, perhaps a fraud – maybe I will be found out. This type of thinking is not only localised to you. All of us, at times, have felt unsure of our place and the contribution we are making to a field. Is it worthwhile? Do we know what we are doing? Will we be 'found out'? Is it really a good idea to expose our ideas and our research to face the possibility of rejection in order to receive the benefit of reaching our final destination? Yes! The path becomes clearer, the navigation more appropriate, the journey easier. But the risk must first be taken ... and then another taken again.



The path that is to be navigated to reach a destination involves the packing of supplies appropriate to the specific journey. It involves journal profiling to ensure the directions are correct. It involves drafting and crafting an article to suit the readership of the journal. It involves alignment of the article's aims and scope with the journal's aims and scope. It involves writing to the conventions of the journal and in the style particular to the journal article genre. Making sure you adhere to the form and content of the particular journal is also very important. For those who know how to do this and have navigated this jungle successfully, their work has been published.

What you must keep in mind is that all feedback received on an article will only help you to improve your thinking and your writing. It will help you to improve as an academic author and researcher. However, negative reviews and critique can be hard to withstand. As I am experienced at receiving rejection, I can claim some authority on the subject!

Some final points about rejection, influenced by Black et al. (1998):

- Your research is not perfect. It has limitations and these should be openly shared.

- You will make mistakes in your work, your writing and in what journal you submit your work. Admit these, learn from them, and move on.

- After you receive rejections, don't be disheartened. 'With perseverance most work can be published somewhere!' (Wager, Godlee and Jefferson 2002: 28). Put your work to the side. Come back to it when you can be more objective.

- Talk about rejection with your colleagues. They will appreciate your candour. It is time to show those skeletons!

- Everyone receives more rejections than they do acceptances.

- Keep writing. While you have one article submitted, be working on another different article.

And, on a final note, which I cannot say any better:

> *It helps to regard getting your work accepted as a game with many variables, where you're constantly trying to make adjustments to your strategy on the basis of experience, and where there is still a considerable element of chance involved. (Black et al. 1998: 100)*



Perhaps I should have titled this book, 'Publishing from Your PhD: A Whole New Ball Game!'

# 8 Thorny Bushes and Muddy Swamps: Things That Slow you Down

In a jungle, there are many hazards. Thorny bushes can traumatise your skin and cut your clothes to shreds. Your progress can be hampered at inopportune moments. Muddy swamps resulting from the constant rain can make each step seem like a painstaking plod. Your time in the jungle is already fraught with challenges. This chapter advises you how to avoid merely trudging or slipping backwards through the jungle.

## JOINT AUTHORSHIP CAN SLOW YOU DOWN OR SPEED YOU UP

While in the social sciences there are many articles that feature only one author, the physical sciences continually demonstrate joint authorship; few papers are published by less than three co-authors (Carolan 2008). Why is there such a sense of camaraderie in the physical sciences, but a demarcation of solo achievement in the social sciences? This is a question I have not yet answered, but it seems that, for many people in the social sciences, they are able to choose whether they go it alone or whether they work with that special colleague with whom they connect.

Many academics speak of the benefits they have received as an individual by working in a group. Others are 'once bitten, twice shy' and are known for their unaccompanied trajectories. Chapters 10–15 (interviews with established academics) provide interesting insight about how team members are sometimes exploited, while also highlighting that the achievement and collaboration of the team is greater than any that could be achieved as an individual. To me, it is about working to your personal strengths. In a team, you could end up doing all the work and get little of the credit. However, there is value in collaboration and joint authorship because both or all members of the team are responsible for the content and then can all contribute to the quality of the article. This can be messy and inequitable, especially if one person lets the team down. But many people prefer to write and research in this way. They enjoy the alliance and association found in the team and relish the feedback, conversation, dialogue and connections made within that environment. They enjoy that each person in the team can contribute to different parts of a journal article, therefore sharing the workload. It seems there are many opportunities for collaboration with people who have an idea, but who need others in order to be effective. If you do not have any innovative ideas on your own, you will need to form a partnership with others.

### Big Picture versus Small Mundane Detail

If you are a big picture person and despise small details, then it may be better for you to work with someone who loves detail. That way, you can complement each other when you submit manuscripts and research grant applications. That said, it is possible to be distracted by fine details; too much attention to them in academia means that you may focus on inconsequential spin-offs, rather than meaningful effects.



## THE UPS AND DOWNS OF GOING IT ALONE

Sole-authored publications carry more weight than joint-authored publications, but may require more time on the part of the individual in order to produce them. If everyone on a team is committed to the project, then there is less effort required from each person compared to if they had to do the whole project or write the whole article themselves. In a team, an article can be produced that utilises the strengths of individuals.

I have actually sought out collaborators for my projects, but have not 'clicked' with anyone in particular. I am still searching and, at the time of publication, seem to have some emerging and promising collaborations. Something that I have perhaps not been so good at, nor placed enough value on, is the benefit of taking time to talk through ideas with colleagues, conceptualising ideas through invigorating discourse. As an early career researcher, there are many obstacles to conducting research within a university environment (life in general!), so it has proved wise to be able to have a senior colleague with whom I can bounce off ideas and check that I am not awry. However, I am not going to wait for that 'special someone' before I go ahead with my ideas and plans. Waiting on a path for the gnats and wasps to get me is not an option.

In keeping with this thinking is the interesting position that is not widely known. It seems that if an idea for a project (input or output) is not 'my idea', then the person whose idea it is is the only one who will be passionate about it. She or he will be the one pushing water uphill, as the mantra for many academics seems to be, 'I am only passionate about what I have thought up.' So, therefore, if you want to work in a team, it appears ideal to generate the chief idea collaboratively so that each team member will have a vested interest and ownership in the project. Being the lead chief investigator (researcher) on a project has status, but it requires a lot more commitment to the project if you do not have the other team members on board. If they do not have the same enthusiasm and familiarity with the project (perhaps because they are wishing to build their own castle, not yours), then you may end up doing the majority of work yourself (along with taking most of the credit). If you are one of the team members, and the 'idea' is not yours, you just have to accept that it is not your idea, and somehow generate the enthusiasm for the project that is needed.



Much value has been placed on interdisciplinary or multidisciplinary collaborations. It is a challenge to form a cohesive group of people that have similar goals in mind with varying perspectives. But as some of the academics featured in this text explain, it is very rewarding.

## THINGS THAT SLOW YOU DOWN

There are many thorny bushes and muddy swamps that can slow you down from progressing through the jungle. Being on committees and organising conferences take you away from writing. Marking enormous numbers of assignments is not valued, even though it should be. While teaching well and giving good feedback to students is beneficial and important, the time it takes must be weighed up against the time it takes to get to your destination in the crowded jungle of publishing your research in academia. Some people do not place value on teaching; they favour their research. Some academics place more value on their teaching and administrative responsibilities to the detriment of their research. It is difficult to be good at everything. But in many instances, you will be able to choose what you get involved in, and how much of any particular task you do. These are crucial decisions as they can affect the time you can give to the activities you truly value.

To me, getting involved in administrative tasks can be good for experience, but I really wonder whether it will help to establish your research career? Will it help to bring about publications? If you can spend more time on your research grant applications and your journal articles that you submit for review, will they not pay off better for you in the long run? There are benefits in knowing how universities operate so you can learn how to operate effectively within them. Knowing how budgets, democracy, management and vision (the big picture) work, as well as dealing with conflict and politics, is seen by some people as invigorating and by others as a drag. If contributing to the life and administration of your faculty is important and expected, it has its pros and cons, because if you do not put your research career first, no one else will. No one else in your faculty will put your career as their number one priority. They have their own careers to think about, and they have their own families to think about. Moreover, it is very easy to be distracted from writing a research grant application or a journal article, or a conference paper in favour of attending to administration, emails, marking and your coffee club. While all these things are important, they could also be considered to be thorny bushes or muddy swamps.

### Not Doing Your Research



If you do not profile the journals which you think you will send your articles to, and if you do not understand what each of them as an entity is about, you are doing yourself a disservice. Your progress will be slow, if at all.

### Submitting Crappy Manuscripts

You set yourself up for failure or for limited progress if you submit a poor quality manuscript for review. Some reviewers will not bother to read beyond the first page if the text is littered with below par grammar, spelling or inadequately constructed sentences. You can always spend more time on journal articles and research grant applications. If you take up that time drinking lots of cappuccinos, your writing will not be as good. Make your time in the jungle count.

## THINGS THAT WILL SPEED YOU UP

Three suggestions for how to speed up your navigation in the jungle now follow.

### Blocking Out Time to Write

An important strategy that will increase your effectiveness and productivity is blocking out or making time to write, that is, working on your research so you can be generating publications (outputs) and successful research grants (inputs). If you do not set aside this time, then you will slow down your progress. Some faculties provide one day a week for a 'research day' whereby you are expected to work away from campus on your research. If you do have this opportunity, make it count. Do not answer emails or do the mundane parts of your job on this day. Do your research and make it a priority.

## Putting Your Curriculum Vitae (CV) First

Professor Sara Dolnicar (see Chapter 15) strongly recommends that, whatever you do, you must put your CV first. She maintains that if you have a traumatic time in your life, this should not be reflected in the output of your CV. In focusing on research as your number one priority, there are some things that must be sacrificed. In recent times, I have been questioning the amount of value I have personally placed on the success of my career. You and I have to determine what cost we will each pay in order to achieve particular goals. Is it worth the stress? Is it worth the long days and nights? Why is it important? What I have recently identified is that I want to decide for myself what my restrictions are, rather than having those restrictions imposed on me by others. To me, if I obtain more research funding and more publications, then I am able, to a certain extent, to distance myself from administrative and vocational demands that may draw me away from focusing on publications. I like the autonomy I receive when I am able to spend time on projects that I see as worthwhile, rather than implementing never-ending policy deemed important by well-meaning bureaucrats. That said, I received an early career teaching award in 2009, and it is something I am proud of, one reason being that teaching students is tangible. You see them every week during the semester and you are dealing with them as people and as individuals. Dealing only with screens, text and theories is not everyone's idea of complete stimulation and has its drawbacks. There is no deadline for the journal article to be submitted, while there is a cut-off date for the lecture to be prepared or the assignments to be marked. It is easy to value the tangible distractions in the jungle.

## An Additional Hazard: Favourites and Being Favoured

As you may have ascertained, citations are very important to an academic. Indeed, Google Scholar can provide you with details of how often articles have been cited and by whom. You do not need to access a library database for the information. However, citations can be positive or negative or be self-citations. The database simply does the counting. This is one way to generate recognition. Esteem and status go alongside this fame. Self-citation is something that I am guilty of (see the references list, for example), not in order to gain more citations, but to hopefully refer readers of my work to other texts that I have produced along similar lines. The cleverly written cartoon titled, 'Your (real) impact factor' (Cham 2008) insinuates that this is not an innocent process. What Cham rightly points to is that, in the demand and ubiquitous pressure to publish, we are expected to perform. It is no wonder that some academics falsely believe that it is acceptable to submit the same version of a published refereed conference paper to a journal for review as an original article.

In the same way, many of the people who I have cited in this manuscript are friends or colleagues. It is because I know them and respect them. It could be claimed that I am being nepotistic in citing Professor Tara Brabazon and Professor Chris Bigum (who are personal friends of mine), and of including academics in this text who I have worked with. Tara Brabazon's work continues to be particularly relevant as she writes about academia and higher education in general. I refer to Chris Bigum's work about Knowledge-Producing Schools a lot in my writing on computers in education because I strongly agree with it. So, I continue to make the point that including known quantities (or qualities) are important. Professor Alison Lee gave me a version of her latest book entitled, *Publishing Pedagogies for the Doctorate and Beyond* (Aitchison, Kamler and Lee 2010), so I have referred to it, not just because I know her, but because it is a significant piece of literature in the field that has been recently released. But because I met her recently and told her about this project, she was able to give me a pre-released PDF of the book so that I would be up to date with current literature. Thank you Alison!



The networking that occurs and who you know will continue to be important as there is a fair element of trust that can be relegated to known persons, and that is worth something to you. I recently contacted an overseas academic whose conference presentation I had attended, because he works in a field that I wish to get into, and I liked the candid nature and quality of his conference presentation. No more than that. I did not even talk to this person individually, but I believe that I can work with him. We plan to work on an international research grant together, albeit virtually for the most part.

So, if you do not know anyone, or you are not continually building your network or multiple networks, and you are not even using virtual communication to connect with people (try www.academia.edu for instance), then your progress will be slowed down. There are many obstacles in the jungle, and 'just' surviving is completely acceptable. But there is much you can do to avoid hampering your progress as you hack your path through the jungle.

# 9 The Final Destination Has Moved, Hack Another Path: The Process of Culling and Prioritising

How do you take a complete whole and cut it into bits? Finished theses range from 80,000 words to 120,000 words or more. Culling the total down to a 4,000-, 6,000-, 8,000- or 10,000-word article is a challenge. This chapter explains the difficulty of taking apart your fascinating findings and explaining them briefly. If your PhD is a complex and substantive document, then there is no doubt that this is a complicated task!

First of all, in putting the thesis together, your advisor or supervisor has encouraged you to ensure that your thesis works as a whole. Right from the introduction throughout the internal chapters to the final conclusion chapter, there is an evident theme or a story that develops from start to finish. Your thesis is encouraged to be a good read – it should have a beginning, middle and end and flow logically from one idea and one section to the next. Your assessor should not have to labour or languish as he or she reads through your carefully articulated prose. So, the mammoth task of obtaining approval to do your research, completing the research, and then writing everything into a cohesive document is not only an enormous mission, but one which takes years to do. It is a significant achievement and, for many, it stops there. That is it. There is nothing left to give. There is no interest in publishing the results. And who can blame them? Receiving a PhD is a magnificent accomplishment. But, for those of us who have chosen the academic path, then we must publish from it, so that we can 'get on our way' through the jungle. But what is firstly involved is a massacre. Your thesis now has to be emasculated. It has to be chopped up in awkward ways, but then each bit then needs to be crafted into its own meaningful 'whole'. It is no wonder that this is difficult.

For some, the thesis is a part of them. Some people hold their thesis close to their body; it is loved and appreciated. Others push their thesis as far away from their body as possible, held with only a finger and thumb in disdain. Dr Julianne Lynch related this applied analogy to me, and I acknowledge that some people cannot wait to be rid of their PhD so they can move onto what they consider to be other, more interesting projects. They despise their PhD as it represents a never-ending torment of sacrifice (or something else negative). But if you are reading this book, that is unlikely to be you. In your eyes, you have worked hard and suffered a lot to get your doctorate so you wish to utilise it. You are proud of the work. You are pleased with what you have said, and you think the research should be published because it is important and makes a contribution. That said, milking it requires more effort and it requires taking apart some of yourself. Your thesis, as a representative of yourself, has to be broken into bits. Luey states:

> *When the dissertation is finished, it can generate articles of a different sort. For example, your dissertation, once stripped of the literature review, methodology, excessive annotation, and the like, may boil down to a single interesting point that can be stated, illustrated, and proved in twenty or thirty pages. That is something to turn into an article. Unfortunately, you usually cannot just take the dissertation and hack it into shape. You should probably start writing from scratch.*
>
> *It is also possible that, with minor revision, a chapter can be turned into an article. Case studies, biographical studies, textual studies, and the like are good candidates. Sometimes a bit of extra research is needed to round out the article.*
>
> *Perhaps nothing in your dissertation can easily be transformed into a publishable article. You may still have material that could be the basis of some good new work that could be completed differently. (2002: 45)*

This is a poignant reminder about the worth of our work. And if you are not ready to consider Luey's suggestions, then it may be time to give your thesis and yourself a rest. I was very enthused about publishing from my PhD and wanted to make the most of it, and do so quickly (I was up for tenure the following year). However, in hindsight, I think I was too close to it and, initially, did not have exactly the right journals in mind.

## THE PATH I NAVIGATED

As I mentioned earlier, in hindsight I wish I had read Day's (2008) and Black et al.'s (1998) books before I even looked at starting to publish from my PhD.

During my PhD candidature, I only presented one poster at a conference about my PhD project. I submitted my thesis in June 2007, and during the second semester of 2007, I extensively worked on one conference paper, and four journal articles based on my PhD.

Each of those five papers described the theoretical framework, methodology and participants in the same way. What was different was the data that was presented. This was influenced in one way because I presented the data and discussion (results and findings) in three themes, one theme per chapter. However, it was not as clear cut as that because each data chapter comprised 10,000 words (one was 12,000 words). The methodology and theoretical section also increased the word count for the possible articles, so I then had to reduce the information to smaller chunks, deciding yet again what to include and exclude.



The first consideration I think is to decide what journal to write for, and then ascertain the word length that your submitted article will have. This is a critical part of the process. For example, two journals that I thought would possibly be interested in publishing my work had a word limit of 6,000 words and 4,000–6,000 words respectively. As I had a 12,000-word draft to start with (taking the theoretical, methodological and one data-themed chapter straight from the thesis), cutting it in half seemed too cutthroat, so therefore the 'market' for my work was narrowed to journals that published lengthier articles.

As I have mentioned, the process of crafting, submitting, reviewing (by others), revising, resubmitting and acceptance took over a year for each journal (see Figure 2.1 on page 20). Yet, had I had the checklists in Chapter 1 and appropriately profiled the journals as per the journal checklist in Chapter 6. I think I would have had less items or points of clarification to revise for resubmission, and subsequently reduced the time for publication. Notably, the hours spent revising the article to suit the journal's expectations would also have been lessened.

## DECIPHERING THE WOOD FOR THE TREES

I am aware of the thinking that states a five-minute speech will be better than a two-hour speech (see Day 2008), and the argument that says you should be able to write the purpose of your article in 20 words or less (Black et al. 1998). I quite enjoy telling my students that just because I do not rave on about something does not mean it is not important. Less is more. So when you go about putting an article together, you have to carefully consider exactly what is going to be said, why it is to be said and why it matters, just like you did with your thesis. However, you have to acutely cull the voluptuous word count into smaller, cohesive segments. This may feel like you have chopped off one of your limbs. But you have to also realise the differences in purpose or focus. As elaborated on in Chapter 3, the thesis and the journal article are completely different beasts.

## WHAT HAVE YOU GOT IN YOUR BACKPACK?

There are various ways to carve up your thesis. But it is an unnatural representation of the whole. If you have been awarded your doctorate, you have reached one destination. In seeking to publish the findings, you then need to decide the best way to distribute your work. As Luey (2002) has suggested, you have the option of rewriting it as a book (or with minimal changes publishing it as a thesis book in the tradition of Verlag) or carving it up into journal articles (perhaps conference papers initially). Whatever you decide, the destination has now changed. If you decide on publishing multiple journal articles from your thesis, you need to acknowledge that there are different conventions and requirements to do so. Chapter 6 details how you can choose the right journal, but you must first decide on your topic and argument. What is it that you want to say and why do you want to say it?



Just to clarify what I described above, my thesis was as follows:

1. Introduction
2. Literature Review
3. Methodology and Research Design
4. Data Theme 1
5. Data Theme 2
6. Data Theme 3
7. Conclusion
8. References.

The findings and discussion were grouped together in each of the three data chapters. Another way to put it is that as I presented the results, I analysed them. I was able to group data into three areas and analyse it with the conceptual framework I employed. More traditional theses might be structured as follows:

1. Introduction

2. Literature Review

3. Methods

4. Findings

5. Discussion

6. Conclusion.



There are of course many alternatives. For me, I thought that if I wrote a journal article about each of the data theme chapters (three in total) that would be ideal. It seemed an appropriate and apt way to carve up the whole. However, what I did not realise at the time was that as each of the data chapters was 10,000–12,000 words, that it would not be an easy 'dump' from one genre to another. When you write an article, it also has to have a beginning, middle and an end, but it is constrained by the word length required by the journal. If the journal's requirements are between 6,000–8,000, then your 12,000-word masterpiece is doomed to only be a gaunt representative of its former self. This is because most journal articles also require an introduction, a literature review, text about the position of the theoretical approach, presentation and discussion about the findings, and a conclusion. You cannot just simply cut a few thousand words from each chapter of your thesis and hope it will be a viable (smaller) whole, or complete version for a journal. In order to work through this difficult challenge, there are a number of strategies you can consider. The interviews with the academics in Chapters 10–15 detail how they went about publishing from their PhD, so those chapters will offer you additional insight to what is presented below.

You may have themes of your data that would be better suited to the audience of an international journal rather than a national one. There may be themes from your data that would be best presented in a journal with a narrow field of focus. The type of methodology and methods used in your study may make a contribution to a journal about research methods. But what you must do before you start writing is a) profile the journal (see Chapter 6), b) decide upon your approach and topic, c) decide on authorship, and then d) go about plotting out your article so that it suits the particular conventions of the journal which you have chosen. There might also be a place to focus on the different audiences, that is, the readership of particular journals. Who reads the journal and why? Do you have something to say to that particular readership?

If you have completed a series of studies within your PhD as a whole, then you may be able to write an article about each study. You may also be able to submit an article based solely on the literature you reviewed for the thesis. If your thesis is constructed in an alternative (non-traditional) way, and you have a number of 'stand-alone' chapters, then you may be able to publish an article from each chapter. Because your thesis is original and unpublished, then you are able to publish these, though you should cite your thesis as the source for these findings. If your thesis is published as a book through Verlag (see Chapter 13 for more detail), then simply it is already published. You must be sure that you still own the copyright to the work, otherwise you will have to rewrite every single sentence so that you are not plagiarising yourself.



Once you have completed the thesis and you are able to state the main finding or insight from the research, you could write what might be considered your main or chief paper from the PhD. This quintessential paper could be the predominant output from your subsequent publications (see Chapter 10). It could be the one that you set aside to submit to an A-star journal. In order to best set yourself up for success, you could present this most important paper at conferences, obtain feedback, rewrite it, enhance it and submit to the most prestigious journal in your field. You may be happy to wait three years for that article to be published, but while you are waiting, you may decide to submit other less important articles from the PhD to A or B or C journals.

You also need to decide on authorship. If you want to co-write with your supervisors or advisors, then it is my opinion that they should make a contribution to the article that you pull from the thesis. Others believe that supervisors' names should be automatically put on manuscripts because they have made contributions to the thesis. But if you are co-authoring, you also need to discuss up front the percentage of authorship and the order of authors on the manuscript.

## THE RUTHLESS ADJUSTMENT

When you write your thesis, you are writing with a few examiners in mind. These examiners will be chosen based on their sympathy to your approach, their interest in the field, their knowledge of the area and their similarly minded worldview. This is no secret. When you send a smaller chunk of your thesis to a journal as an article, the reviewers will be chosen because of their expertise and experience, and will be expected to complete a blind review. They do not know who you are, nor do they care. They are there to do a job, a good one hopefully, and they are usually under pressure to do so. Reviewers are not chosen because they sympathise with your paradigm, because they like your methodology or because they think you are a great person. They are given a job to do, that of assessing the quality of the article, its argument and the rigour of the research. You need to keep this in the forefront of your mind. For the thesis, you wrote for a narrow audience, but when writing journal articles, you are now trying to largely appeal to a wider group of people. Your writing needs to reflect this. It needs to be concise, complete and thorough, but it also needs to leave out unnecessary prose which may be important to the production of the thesis, but is not of value to the genre of a journal article.



What remains evident is that you need to figure out what your main findings are, and where they should be published. These main points also need to link to the literature that you have reviewed and be current with contemporary discourse. Therefore, this involves knowing a lot about possible avenues for publication (see Chapter 6). Having a portfolio approach is one way. Identify the main finding for a high status output, and then assign the other not so important findings to less esteemed outlets. Another option is to do as I did, where I did not place more value on one finding over another, but simply wanted to get as many outputs as possible in the best journals that would accept them. I focused on researching where I thought would be a suitable avenue of acceptance, then crafting the article for that journal. This required many rewrites and edits. I did what the reviewers asked as best as I could and I ended up publishing four journal articles, one refereed conference paper and one book from my PhD. Each of these outputs made important points from my PhD, and I do not consider one paper to be better than another, but what is evident is that the A-star journal publication is more prestigious than some of the other outputs. And while I can say I have written a book, I am unsure as to how widely it has been distributed, whereas online access to journal articles means that publications can be extensively diffused.

## THE NEW PATHWAY

As you remind yourself you have a new destination, you will be able to set your sights on hacking suitable and multiple paths towards this destination. You are now prepared to decipher the wood for the trees and you have plenty of supplies in your backup. But before you set off on your own, it is apt you learn some more about others' trials during their journeys through the jungle.

# Prologue:
# Introducing the Interviews with the Academics

I am quite prepared to accept the criticism that this book only includes academics who are, or have recently been, employed at the University of Wollongong, New South Wales, Australia, and that in order for it to be more applicable and appropriate, there should be interviews included from people from other universities in different countries. I did wonder about whether this was a limitation, but based on the interviews presented in the following chapters (in no particular order), I can confidently say that there are multiple perspectives presented by the academics featured in this book. They each contribute a qualitatively different approach as to how to go about publishing, and it truly makes for fascinating reading.

I hope you enjoy the richness of insight that is presented in the following pages by these experienced, successful academics who have international profiles. I purposely chose to include their interviews verbatim so that their words, and their thoughts could be imparted on paper, to show the depth and breadth of viewpoints surrounding publishing within the jungle of academia. The other purpose of including their words verbatim was to demonstrate that they are real people who do speak normally, but they have studied and excelled in the art of academic writing and academia in general.

The manifold and global perspectives that are expressed in the following chapters demonstrate a mixture of ways of looking at the process of reviewing and the political challenges that are faced when negotiating the jungle of academia. Professor Jan Herrington's work mainly lies in higher education and educational technology, specifically authentic learning. Professor Paul Chandler is well known for his work on cognitive load theory from the field of the learning sciences. Professor Lori Lockyer's specialty is in learning objects and learning designs. Professor Jan Wright's areas of interest broadly include gender and physical education. Professor Wilma Vialle's work focuses on gifted education and multiple intelligences. Professor Sara Dolnicar is a specialist in tourism and marketing.

I acknowledge that other areas of the social sciences are not included, for instance, philosophy, literature, languages and the creative arts. But the insights that are shared in the following chapters can be applied to various fields. With that in mind, I am sure that the subsequent prose will prove valuable to you.

# 10 Professor Jan Herrington

Professor Jan Herrington is based in the School of Education at Murdoch University, Perth, Western Australia. She was formerly an English high school teacher in Victoria, and an instructional designer in multimedia at Edith Cowan University, Western Australia. Jan was only awarded her PhD in 1998, so her meteoric rise to professorship is notable (similar to some of the other professors featured in this book). In 2002, Jan received the Fulbright Scholarship award to conduct research in the United States, from the Australian-American Fulbright Commission. From 1998–2008, she attracted more than AUD$800,000 in research and teaching funding. Her much anticipated book, entitled *A Guide to Authentic e-Learning*, was released in 2009 (Herrington, Reeves and Oliver 2009). Jan's other well-known books include *Effective Use of the Internet: Keeping Professionals Working in Rural Australia* (Herrington and Herrington 2006a), *Authentic Learning Environments in Higher Education* (Herrington and Herrington 2006b), and the recent electronic book, *New Technologies, New Pedagogies: Mobile Learning in Higher Education* (Herrington et al. 2009).

Alongside the outstanding book count (14), Professor Herrington has authored more than 35 refereed journal articles and 90 refereed conference papers, and has received a number of outstanding conference paper awards. She is an immensely popular and successful keynote speaker. In this chapter, Jan shares how she has made the most out of publishing from her PhD.

## PROFESSIONAL DIALOGUE

**NICOLA Hi Jan, when and where did you receive your PhD [doctorate in philosophy]?**

JAN I studied at Edith Cowan University, and I finished the PhD in 1997 and was awarded it in 1998.

**NICOLA How many publications did you get out of the PhD [entitled, *Authentic Learning in Interactive Multimedia Environments*]?**

JAN Many, many, I have to say, and not just on the completed PhD, but all the way through. So I was publishing on the substance of the PhD from the first model, which I'd put together from situated learning. This then created the basis for the software that we developed in a situated learning model and then we implemented and evaluated it in a design-based research approach. So [I published] right from that first literature review and those elements which eventually became my model of authentic learning. It was published at the ascilite conference [Australasian Society for Computers in Learning in Tertiary Education] and in fact, that's still one of my most cited works, interestingly.



At every phase, there were many publications about the methodology or a small part of the methodology. For instance, I used a piece of software at the time called 'Video search'. It's now been commercialised as a qualitative analysis tool with video data, so I used a very early prototype of that to analyse what happened when students used this program, which we had developed based on the situated learning model. The students were given a task and used the program, and we videotaped them as they worked, and then I analysed what they did as they worked with the program. A lot of computer-based programs up to that point had been just click and point, rapid response, where you didn't have to think much. So I took a short video of the data. I only analysed 30 minutes because that was the cutting edge of the technology. You had to have huge external memory drives, just to be able to do it. But that was fantastic because we analysed it according to whether students were attending, whether they were conversing, whether they were just sitting there looking, whether they were writing on the computer, and so on. So that was another paper I did with the author of the software.

There were nine elements of authentic learning and there are two chapters of literature review in my thesis. One was generally of the whole area under investigation, the second chapter was taking each of those nine elements and doing a short literature review of each of those, so in fact, I found that I then had nine, almost discrete literature reviews of aspects of situated learning. For instance, collaboration had its own literature review, articulation had its own literature review, authentic assessment had its own, so that was the basis of many useful publications. So it was like I 'mined' that thesis, in fact, I kept a copy of it [and] called it a 'monitoring copy'. If I had used a paragraph of the thesis, I'd underline or highlight in some way the paragraphs I had actually used. I have always been pretty careful not to plagiarise myself which probably is a bit silly but, wherever I could, I tried to only use a paragraph once. But of course when I referred to the nine elements, I would repeat those every time if it was relevant, but I usually cite the original publication. I really was keen to use as much of the thesis as I could because if you've got really good literature on collaboration or whatever, why not use it?

**NICOLA So you wanted to make the most of how much work you'd put into the thesis?**

JAN Yes, exactly, and in fact, in terms of publishing from a whole thesis, there were four studies within the thesis, and each one of those was published. There was also an overall paper with my supervisor that covered the whole thesis, and I'd say that is my main publication. It was published in a top tier US journal and that's still my most cited paper. That was published in 2000.



**NICOLA Now is that the one where you had the numerous reviews?**

JAN Yes, indeed. There was a competition run by an educational technology association for the best new research. I submitted a paper on my research and it was reviewed by four judges (I think) and I won the competition. Part of the prize was that the winner gave a special invited presentation and was invited to submit a shorter version of the paper to an affiliated journal for review. So this of course was just absolutely wonderful, to have just finished my PhD and win this prize and get published in a high-quality journal. But then, the next thing – I received a letter in the mail to say, 'Thank you for your submission but it's been rejected' and honestly, I had to sit down. I could not believe it because I thought this was part of the prize!

Shortly afterwards I went to a conference, and caught up with some people associated with the competition. They were also shocked to hear that the paper had been rejected. One then took it up with the editor of the journal who then wrote back to me and asked me to revise it, and it went out to review again. So it went to another three reviewers, different ones, and then it went to another three and so they all came back with reviews suggesting changes, with many suggestions directly contradictory to others.

So I revised it and sent it back to the editor and he then sent the paper back to the same three reviewers that had reviewed it the first time. It was so interesting because the final published paper was very close to the original paper. It was like we were playing a game.

Eventually it got accepted and it was published and I think it is one of their well-cited papers in that journal. The experience was very crushing though for a new researcher, and I wonder if I did not have contacts to support my case whether it would ever have been published.

**NICOLA So all up, what was the total amount of reviews on the paper?**

JAN There were 21 reviews in all.

**NICOLA Wow. So how did you divide up your thesis? You've talked a little bit about how you went about publishing, but with your nine elements, you've basically published a paper on each of the elements?**



JAN There's one area which I haven't actually published but I've put it in my book now <laughing> (Herrington, Reeves and Oliver 2010).

**NICOLA So do you have a total of how many publications from your PhD?**

JAN Ah, I could add it up for you but honestly it's been the basis for quite a lot of the work that I've done, apart from some of the stuff I've done on communities of practice. Oh there are probably a few areas of research I've explored that don't cover it. But the thesis really created the model for me. I'm always invited to speak about authentic learning. The only time I haven't used it in a keynote was AARE [Australian Association for Research in Education conference] in Fremantle (2007). That was the one time that I'd been invited to speak about research, not specifically authentic learning or authentic assessment.

So if you can, I think you should create an area in which you can become the expert, or use your degree to research something that's sustainable, that's going to give you a reputation for being the expert in that field rather than merely adequate. It shows that there's been good research training rather than really creating the area that you've now made your own that you can now use as a springboard to go into academia. But you see from the PhD research, with my co-researchers I then won two [nationally competitive grants]. So the thesis was the starting point but from that I've really built on it.

**NICOLA So what were some difficulties you faced in publishing from your PhD?**

JAN Well apart from that journal article, I'd have to say publishing has been quite straightforward. I've tended to use the established route that we use as academics, where you put your work up for a conference, which typically is easier to get accepted, and you present the paper. You get feedback from the conference paper review, you get feedback from the presentation itself and then you can work on that, possibly with another conference paper to write a journal article. I think there are not too many conference papers that can go straight to publication in a journal. Mind you, there are international conferences where, if you are highly reviewed, or say you get an outstanding paper [award], you get invited to publish in one of their journals. It gets reviewed in the knowledge that this was a highly regarded paper at a conference. So I find if you follow that route then you're given feedback and support all the way along rather than say picking say a top tier journal and going for that.



**NICOLA So you found that the process you're referring to is quite tried and true and it just helps you to continually improve it throughout the process of writing it and to submission?**

JAN Yes I think so, and I think that that's what we as a community do. We're then drawing on all that knowledge that's in our community, through the reviewing process, through the public presentation and public defence of ideas to really help to shape up a work so that it is not raw. Then by the time you submit it to a journal you've got something that's already been reviewed and reflected upon and polished and improved to the point where it's going to be harder to reject.

**NICOLA What are the memorable experiences you had as an early career academic?**

JAN Well there was winning that competition – that was just an outstanding thing for an early career academic. In 2002 – this is one of the really great things that happened to me – I applied for a Fulbright scholarship. I just saw it advertised in the *Campus Review*. I just thought 'Yes go for it.' And then in December, I got home from work one day and there was an envelope from the Fulbright Association, and it was a big fat envelope – it wasn't just a little tiny letter – so I knew I had won it. I got to travel to the United States for up to four months. We had to organise special visas and the whole family came with me, the kids went to school in American schools. We lived in the community in the States and easily, that was just the best thing that happened to me in my early career. I encourage my students now to apply for these awards and competitions to recognise the quality of what they've done. It's a good way to get your work recognised and really start to [build your] professional profile. I think you have to go after these opportunities, you have to pursue them. Don't think you can just sit back and wait for things to fall in your lap.

**NICOLA Would you say it's safe to say that you get better at knowing what you have to do to make a journal article accepted?**

JAN Yes, yes absolutely. Another thing that I'd recommend people do is review for journals and conferences because in reviewing you're sharpening your critical approach and you learn what makes a good written paper. If you review a paper and it just launches straight in to a description of a project and says something like, 'We had an idea, we did a course in x, or we thought we would try a new multimedia approach', you know instantly that this is not enough for a scholarly paper. You would find yourself asking, 'Where's the literature, where's the theoretical framework for this, is this just an idea that's plucked out of the air?' So with experience, you can very quickly recognise the faults, and can bring that to bear on your own writing. The more you review, the more you recognise the formula for doing a good written paper.



**NICOLA Have you something to say about the subjectivity of review, for example, discrepant reviews?**

JAN Oh yes, it's amazing to me how discrepant they can be and how directly contradictory they can be. I find that with many reviews, often the editors will summarise the reviews before sending them back to you, but if you were able to read them raw, quite often the reviewer is just spouting off and letting their own prejudices come through, hiding behind their anonymity. But then sometimes you'll get a really good, thoughtful review where a reviewer has said, 'This has not been justified well' and you think to yourself, 'Yes that's right I haven't argued that very well' and the paper is really improved as a result of that feedback. And often with misunderstandings, I think you'll just have to acknowledge that this is the way that a reviewer has read your writing. You may not agree with them but you have to accept that that's how they have read and interpreted it, so it's not quite clear the way you've expressed it – and that in itself is good feedback.

**NICOLA What types of things can slow academics down in terms of progress and publications?**

JAN As academics we don't get the time that we need to do quality research. We should be contributing to knowledge about how people learn and how we can improve that and we just don't get the time. We're bound down by so many teaching-related or administrative activities. That sounds really terrible because I do really believe that teaching is our main job, and it needs to come first. But our teaching needs to be informed by our research and I think our research always gets put on the back burner. We do it when we've got time and that's after marking assignments. The amount of time we get – I just have to laugh at the amount of time we get – we get 15 minutes to mark an assignment. Some of the ones we mark in the technology subjects, you couldn't even put the CD in the computer and figure out mentally where you have to go before the 15 minutes is up, before you've even looked at any of the work on the CD. Some of these assignments can take one to two hours to mark. So those sorts of things really do impact on research and it's almost like your research becomes your optional activity that you do over and above your job. I think that's sad that that's happened.



Progress will be slow if you fail to have a clear idea in any one year about which conferences you're going to go to. I think the conference timetable really helps to keep you on track. I like to go to one conference where papers are due in December and so I work towards a December deadline. So I think that's really handy. I think it's important to want to go to conferences and find the time to submit papers to refereed conferences – there's no point going to all that effort to do something that's not refereed. So, yes that can slow you down if you fail to think and plan ahead what you're going to, and what your output is going to be in any one year.

I'd recommend people try to always have about three or four journal articles in contention at any one time. So you don't just put one in and then wait and see if that gets published because that might happen two or three years down the track. It's just ridiculous how long it takes sometimes, but just make sure that there's a steady flow. I aim to do about 12 co-authored conference papers and four journal articles a year. Usually I don't complete that many but that's what I aim for. Once you start working on a few projects and writing with your students, you have many publishing opportunities.

**NICOLA I had no idea that you went to 12 different conferences?**

JAN No, it wouldn't be 12 conferences, it would be 12 papers, so you might have two PhD students and then a paper of your own so that's three at the one conference. Very rarely would I go to a conference and only do one paper.

**NICOLA So how many conferences would you go to in a year?**

JAN I would aim for two or three, plus any keynotes or invited presentations. Often when you do a keynote the organisers ask you to do a workshop as well so you get to disseminate your work through a workshop.

**NICOLA In terms of slowing down one's progress, I'm choosing not to get involved on committees and extra tasks and administration. Do you think that's a good thing?**

JAN Definitely, this is what I always say to my PhD students, make your PhD the number one priority for you, and work on it every day. Keep the research theme foremost in your mind. Some activities though are very professionally rewarding, for instance, doing reviewing for conferences and journals. If you can apply to be on a committee like that, you get to meet a whole lot of other people that are from all over the world, you're opening up your networks, your name is becoming known as being associated with this endeavour, so I think definitely things like that are good, but not while you are doing your PhD. Save this for when you have finished. If you get involved in too much at the university level, for instance a student or elected representative on committee X, you are losing sight of the main goal. I think give those a miss, unless you can see that you're going to learn quite a lot, in terms of professional learning or research conduct. But I wouldn't go on a committee to discuss space utilisation or something like that unless it related to your research area.

**NICOLA Well, thank you very much Jan.**

JAN Oh, it's a pleasure.

# 11 Professor Paul Chandler

Professor Paul Chandler is currently the Dean of the Faculty of Education, University of Wollongong, and was formerly the Head of School of Education at the University of New South Wales, Sydney. During his career, Paul has attracted more than AUD$2.3 million in research funding and has published more than 30 refereed articles in high-impact international journals. He is regarded as an international expert in cognition and learning. He received his PhD from the University of New South Wales and from this thesis received numerous awards and grants, was invited to deliver keynote addresses in Europe and the USA, and published the findings in three high-impact international journals. Paul has received numerous national and international research awards. In 1992, he became the first education academic to receive an Australian Research Council (ARC) postdoctoral research fellowship. He is currently the most cited educational researcher appointed at any Australian university. In 2008, at a National Press Club event, Professor Chandler was recognised as one of Australia's ten most pre-eminent researchers.

Paul grew up in Sydney and was the first person in his family to receive any formal education beyond primary school. From there he went on to complete high school and also teach high school mathematics and science in his community after completing his undergraduate studies. Paul is involved in a host of community initiatives that help disadvantaged youth in the areas of health and education and is deeply committed to making a difference in the early years. He sits on the board of numerous 'not for profit' organisations while still maintaining a highly active role nationally in teacher education and internationally as a researcher. In this chapter, Paul outlines the benefits of publishing during your PhD candidature, and highlights the benefits of critical engagement.

## PROFESSIONAL DIALOGUE

**NICOLA How did you go about publishing the findings from your PhD?**

PAUL I had a clear strategy. I believe in publishing while you're enrolled in a PhD so I went about my publishing while I was doing my PhD by ascertaining when I thought there was a reasonable contribution to the field and when there was something innovative that was shown in the research. So I submitted articles before the PhD was completed.



By going through that review process, you can professionally develop as a PhD writer. So if you've got a thick enough skin, then by going through the review process, you can build on what is contained in the PhD. That's one part, it's part of your own professional development which I found very rewarding, also extremely challenging. When findings are important, you may as well publish and not wait until the thesis is done.

**NICOLA So did you end up doing a thesis by publication?**

PAUL No, I did a more conventional thesis. Publication during a thesis was my strategy and I think that would serve early career researchers very well. [There is a tendency] in education, arts and associate sciences to publish after your thesis. I feel with the demands of modern academia that it is much more in the interests of professional development to start thinking about publishing during your PhD. This won't be appropriate for all PhDs, obviously, because some need to be looked at holistically or in their complete nature so it won't be appropriate for all. But if I had my time again, I'd do it exactly the same again and I encourage all my PhD students to do that as well.

**NICOLA So what were some difficulties you faced in publishing from your PhD?**

PAUL I was very lucky to publish in the best international journals in my field. What were the challenges? Personally dealing with the reviewers' reports as an early career researcher can be very crushing experiences. They can be very humbling, and unless you're equipped with a supportive network, you can be very dismayed by the reports. The reviewer's report is the most challenging part, but where the challenge lies is also the opportunity. From publishing out of my PhD I learnt a lot about all those qualities of being adaptable, being flexible, being able to formulate arguments. It is a personal challenge to take on board a reviewer's comment and not take it personally. I feel that one of the things that gets lost in academia sometimes is that the publishing process becomes very personal. I think that one needs to separate themselves from the research and to look upon it saying these are some comments that are about my research, not of me.

**NICOLA Have you an anecdote that you can share about a frustrating experience about publishing in a journal?**

PAUL Yes, the greatest frustration that I ever had publishing was actually my greatest triumph. My major article that came out of my PhD was submitted to the leading international journal in learning. It was savaged by the reviewers but the experiments, the results from the studies were that remarkable that the editor of the journal thought it may be worth publishing. So it was sent out for further reviews. The reviewers were mixed but all demanded the right to critique the article publicly but we [the authors] were allowed to write a reply in the same journal issue. That was very challenging. I didn't understand the ferocity of the opposition to my work. I couldn't understand the personal tone of the reviewers' reports so that was challenging. Out of it came the triumph. What would have been yet another obscure article in another journal read by one or two people suddenly became very prominent. In fact, that article became the basis of many awards, fellowships and research accolades that followed many years later. Since then maybe 15, 20 years down the track I've actually met the reviewers and shook their hands and thanked them for the great career [laughing]. The most heavy critics of my research turned out to be the most helpful and provided me with frank feedback and the opportunities to grow as a researcher.



**NICOLA OK, thinking back over your career is there a memorable experience you can share as an early career academic?**

PAUL Many experiences. The collegiality of working with other early career researchers is the greatest part of research. [At that time], you have some of the best ideas, you can't ever undervalue that part of your life. The most important part of the whole journey is engaging with other early career researchers – particularly when you're all PhD students – engaging [with] and knowing about each other's research. I think that students need to move away from being under the feet of their supervisors. Supervisors are certainly a crucial part of the research training, but collegiality and the engagement of other researchers who work in the area is where you grow as a researcher. So having the strong engagement of other career researchers who are on the same trajectory was great; also having a very supportive supervision team. I think that's crucial. So my best memories are of sitting around with other PhD students, arguing out research, having a good and critical research engagement at a broader level, not just my own research. I think that one of the things that you can fall into is the trap of thinking that your own PhD research is the only thing of importance in the field. The best experiences are learning what other people are doing as well.

**NICOLA So leading on from that, what advice would you give to early career researchers?**

PAUL OK, my advice to early career researchers is, 'Don't just look for the affirmations'. I think from my own experience, the affirmations are all well and good but where I believe one grows as a researcher is from the constructive, critical engagement. I think that is still the key to and will always be the key to bettering yourself as a researcher. It's not [about] surrounding yourself by an affirmation group but seeking out wider networks to have people constructively engage in research and critically engage in research. I really think that that is where you grow as a researcher. I never learned anything from somebody who told me how good my research was, I always learnt more from people who would tell me how bad it was.



**NICOLA What would you say about your observations about the process of getting published in journals, especially prestigious ones?**

PAUL My view is 'aim high'. I think in educational research, nationally and internationally, we don't aim high enough. This is determined by a lot of factors, things like probation [tenure], promotion. We tend to be obsessed with the quantity of publications and funding sometimes tends becomes the determiner of your behaviour. We need to have a real alignment on the quality of our work. My advice for early career researchers is to aim high, and go for the prestigious journals but in doing so knowing that it's going to be a longer process. Know that it's going to be a more challenging process; know that you're going to come off with a lot more bumps and bruises than what you will going [with] the non-prestigious journals.

**NICOLA So for those people who are just starting out and they don't feel like they've got that support network, what would your advice be to them?**

PAUL Start seeking out those like-minded souls. Some early career researchers and some institutions are isolated. What they need to do is to form networks, work in teams, work with leaders in the field and start to publish with them. Having good mentors – your good mentor may lie in your faculty, she/he may well lie in some other part of your institution, or may well lie in some other university nationally or internationally. There are many people with whom you can build relationships As an early career researcher I actively sought them out, researchers from Europe and northern America, to take my research to the next level.

**NICOLA So what can early career researchers expect from submitting articles to journals for review?**

PAUL Journal publication is not the holy grail. What you learn from doing it is the most important thing. What you learn from it, you don't learn from a non-review process – you don't learn to grow at the same rate as a researcher. Throughout the process, publication in a journal is a growing experience. You look at how other people's frames of references cast upon your research and in that way, as I said before, you become adaptable because you start separating yourself from the path, the article, and start looking at the research from the outsiders' perspective. So that's what I think you get from journal publications that you don't get in other non-review mechanisms and I really think that's an important part.



**NICOLA What types of things can slow academics down in terms of progress and publications?**

PAUL Submitting to journals with slow turnaround times. Do your research first.

**NICOLA You've had a meteoric rise in your career, how would you suggest that other people go about a meteoric rise like you have had?**

PAUL Oh, look, it was a combination of good fortune, ability and a fantastic supervisor, the best. I would like to attribute it all to my ability but that would be incorrect. It's a matter of good fortune, [and the] ability to believe in yourself and do high-quality work. Never let your ego get in the way of your career. Be willing to learn off anybody but then also go the extra yards networking, going out there and meeting people, learning from lots of people, and never being afraid to go outside your comfort zone. I have been fortunate to achieve all these things. I am proud of being Australia's most cited educational researcher and I am proud of being all the other firsts in Australia, Australia's first ARC Education Post Doctoral Fellow, and so on. I don't see them as milestones, I basically see them as the reward for engaging in all these sort of behaviours, but yeah, be guided by many and not by one, that's my belief.

**NICOLA That's great, thanks, it's a great place to end.**

# 12 Professor Lori Lockyer

Professor Lori Lockyer originates from Toronto, Canada and moved to Australia in 1997 to commence her doctoral candidature. After graduating she decided to take up a full-time academic position and is now the Associate Dean (Research and Graduate) in the Faculty of Education. Her field of specialty is educational technology, and her focus has included, but is not restricted to, research on using technology to support health and medical education. Since 1994, she has attracted more than AUD$3.4 million dollars in research funding from competitive funding schemes and industry.

One of her many awards includes the 2008 Platinum Learning Impact Award from the IMS Global Learning Consortium (with Martin Olmos) for the Online Learning Environment of the Graduate School of Medicine (established in 2007) at the University of Wollongong. Lori has published more than 20 refereed journal articles and more than 50 refereed conference papers. She recently co-edited and released the two-volume *Handbook of Research on Learning Design and Learning Objects* (Lockyer et al. 2008). She is known for her multidisciplinary work and collaboration, and is an editorial board member of the *Journal of Interactive Learning Research* and the *International Journal for Learning Technology*.

In this chapter, Lori discusses the benefits of co-authorship and collaboration with other researchers, including your supervisors. She highlights some strategies about how it is possible to publish during your doctoral candidature. Lori also provides useful insight into the journal reviewing process.

## PROFESSIONAL DIALOGUE

**NICOLA Lori, first of all when and where did you receive your PhD?**

LORI University of Wollongong and I received my PhD in 2000.

**NICOLA And how many publications did you get out of your PhD?**

LORI Two journal articles, two fully refereed conference papers, and I [think] about six conference presentations.

**NICOLA So how many of those were published during your candidature or were they all afterwards?**

LORI Most of them were during. One journal article was during and one was after. One journal article was requested by an editor after having seen one of my conference presentations. He requested that I submit for a special issue of the journal that he was editing, which was looking at a particular focus in terms of higher education, which was the setting of my research. So the journal article went through the peer review process but I hadn't been aware of the call for papers for that special issue before I was approached by the editor. So that was published about a year before I submitted my thesis.



The refereed conference presentations were before I graduated. One of them was within the first year – at the time that I was engaged in data collection and some preliminary analysis. One of them was after I had completed the study and written most of the thesis.

The other conference presentations were for a variety of audiences. So these were presentations where the abstract would have been reviewed but a situation where they didn't have full, refereed conference proceedings. In my area of educational technology most conferences have full, refereed conference proceedings but there were some areas where I thought it was important to attend the conferences and be able to talk about and get feedback on my work. So the publication wasn't as much of an issue for me. I did those progressively through my study. Also, at the end of the study, a 'new thing' called online conferences started and I thought given that my area was online learning, it would be a good idea for me to have the experience of presenting in an online conference. So that was an example of something that I thought was important to do during the course of my study.

**NICOLA How did you divide up your thesis into articles or conference papers?**

LORI Some of the first writing and presentations that I did were more about the idea of my study – so an extended research proposal. I also talked about how I was analysing data with some preliminary analysis, and how I was looking at my study. The reason I was interested in publishing as I went along was to be able to get some feedback. For me conference presentations and journal writing was about getting feedback from a range of people.

In your PhD experience, obviously you have supervisors who are giving you detailed feedback throughout the process. But I think it is important to get feedback from a wide range of people, people who have different expertise, people who might understand different contexts, and be able to help you think a little bit differently about your study and how it might be relevant to other situations. So initially, presenting was about the ideas behind my study and how I was engaged with the ideas.

The journal articles were focused on the findings of my study. Initially, the first journal article was some preliminary analysis around the learning outcomes. The second journal article was focused on the overall results of my study. My study focused on outcomes of knowledge, attitude and behaviour change. It was a study about online learning and involved looking at these outcomes as well as the nature of the online discourse. It also focused on students' perspective because online learning was new in the late 90s. So students' perspectives on the experience was a novel thing at the time in terms of research – the second journal article also reported on these student perspectives.



In terms of the extent of publications on my PhD, I could have published more from my PhD, maybe some more conceptual work based on the literature and some of the ideas initially from the study, or focused particularly on the discourse analysis that was related to my findings. But I moved on from my PhD study into some follow-on studies very quickly. So some of the findings from my PhD ended up translating into other publications where I pulled findings from it and findings from the follow-on studies. Some of the subsequent publications in terms of journal articles, book chapters and conference publications in the two years after I completed my PhD, would have brought my literature and findings from my PhD study as well as literature findings from other studies that I was doing and combine them together into publications.

**NICOLA I think you're a strong advocate of collaboration and joint authored publications, so could you talk a little bit about how the ones we were talking about that are directly from your PhD – were they sole authored?**

LORI I included my two supervisors as co-authors in all of my refereed publications because they contributed to the actual writing of the articles. I guess it depends a bit on the supervisory relationship and how much detailed involvement your supervisors have in advising on your study. My supervisors, I felt, contributed significantly in the design of my study. They provided feedback as I analysed data and on drafts of my thesis. So I didn't even think twice about including them in the writing of the publications. I didn't consider that I would only have a sole-authored publication out of my PhD. I guess I acknowledge their involvement throughout the PhD process and therefore recognised that they would be helpful in the writing of the publications out of the PhD.

Also, my research training before my PhD was in a research institute where collaborators contributed in every project which I was involved. I have had others invite me to contribute to their studies and I have invited others to contribute to studies which I have initiated. Often that's been because I've been involved in multidisciplinary projects so people bring different perspectives in terms [of] design, analysis and writing about a study.



**NICOLA So regarding the subsequent studies of which your PhD led into, did you continue the collaboration with your supervisors or did you try to get other people involved?**

LORI Both. There were a range of projects that I have been involved in and it depended on the nature of the project and the [level of] interest.

**NICOLA So what have been some difficulties you've faced in publishing from your PhD?**

LORI The hardest aspect of peer review, whether it is for publications or research grant applications, is putting your ego on the line for feedback. If it's a good peer review process, you will get detailed feedback that highlight the limitations and constructively provide suggestions. So any kind of difficulty I experienced was learning to cope with the feedback that you get – not so much rejection, but learning to cope with criticism. But, in the main, I found that feedback is constructive and when you take it on board it does mean that what you write about is better or the study idea that you develop is better. But when you first receive that kind of feedback, learning to deal with critical analysis of your work is a skill that as an academic we all have to develop. I don't think it ever goes away no matter how many times you've been rejected or you get critical feedback <laughing>.

In terms of difficulties – I think for academics in general, particularly those who are teaching/research academics – is the time it takes for writing and publication and the turnaround time for publications. In my particular situation, during and immediately after my PhD studies, I was also a casual lecturer research assistant involved in a number of other projects. So that meant that the amount of time I spent publishing about my PhD work was limited. I was teaching, working on research projects and co-authoring articles about those projects while I was working on my PhD study and trying to write articles about it.

**NICOLA So what is a memorable experience you've had as an early career academic?**

LORI My best experience I had <laughing> was finding out that I had been awarded a nationally competitive research grant within three years after finishing my PhD. I got the grant as the lead chief investigator. I had been successful as a co-chief investigator previously, which was a really great experience. But being a lead was an even better experience – particularly being the lead on a multidisciplinary grant that involved academics in three different faculties. It also involved industry support, so negotiating with industry representatives to work through a research idea that was suitable, that was appropriate, that was worthy. I guess I felt it was the first significant achievement I had beyond my PhD. One of my early research mentors talks about the PhD as a licence, like a driver's licence. I never saw the completion of my PhD as the ultimate goal of my career, [it] just gave me the ticket to go on to be a researcher. So I think the most memorable experience was the day I found out that I got that research grant as a lead – I felt that was a significant achievement, that all the work that I'd done on my PhD <laughing> and all the knowledge and skills I had developed through that process had put me into a place that I could move forward.



**NICOLA So would that be your experience that was really a surprise or good fortune or is there something else that you can share that was maybe not expected?**

LORI During my PhD studies I had the good fortune of getting scholarships. When I had made a decision to undertake my PhD, I had been working in a research institute for three years and really began to enjoy research but realised that if I wanted to go further with research I had to do my PhD – I had to get that driver's licence. So it was a hard decision but I quit a very good job, a job I enjoyed immensely and moved to the other side of the world and became a poor starving student <laughing> to do my PhD. The timing was such that I had missed out on applying for scholarships so I just enrolled in the PhD and didn't really worry too much about how I was going to pay for my tuition and feed myself as an international student. I just figured I'd find part-time work to do that. Subsequent to being enrolled in a PhD, I received scholarships – one was particularly competitive from a national research funding body. So this was the surprise because I applied not expecting to get it. So when I did, I didn't have to worry so much about how I was going to pay my fees and put food on the table. But it also meant that it helped start my track record for me of being able to demonstrate the ability to get funding. So I think that's another aspect of research training for people.

I think an aspect of the PhD process, and the research training process, is understanding the different reward systems in academia, and the indicators of quality. Awards, research grants, scholarships ... so finding those kinds of opportunities and applying for those opportunities [is important], even if they seem like a long shot. That made a difference for me in helping to kickstart my early academic career.



**NICOLA Have you an anecdote you can share about a frustrating experience about publishing in a journal?**

LORI A frustrating experience is one I've had several times and many years subsequent to my PhD, so it doesn't just happen to naive career researchers. A lot of the process of publication [in] journals is about doing as much research as you can about the journal and see how your study fits, or can be positioned to fit, into the scope of the journal. I think that's something that I have had to learn over time and I've had to learn some strategies to try to identify if it's an appropriate venue. One of those strategies is sending an abstract of an article to an editor to get a sense of whether the article will fit with the journal after having done the research about the journal in the scope of the journal. I've had a couple of incidences over the years where I've done that. I've got a sense from the editor that based on the abstract the article is appropriate for the journal. Then after you go to the trouble of finessing the article to meet the criteria of the journal even further, you then get some feedback returned that really no; it's not within the scope of the journal. So I think that would probably be the most frustrating experience that I've had in terms of receiving feedback back from journals. I don't know if the issue is that the abstract hasn't been written well enough to really describe the extent of the paper and how it's positioned, or if it's the busy time frame that journal editors are working within.

**NICOLA So would you agree with the statement that most common rejections of articles are usually to do because it doesn't fit with the journal's range and scope?**

LORI I don't know if I could agree with that. As a member of editorial boards and a referee for journals, I have rejected a lot of articles where I thought the scope was fine but the quality of the paper wasn't there and sometimes the quality of the study itself wasn't there. Sometimes the quality is such that no matter how extensive your feedback is, it will seemingly never get up to scratch for the journal. So I don't know if it's just about scope.

**NICOLA So what would your advice be if you could have a soapbox to say to early career researchers, 'This is my advice', what would you say?**

LORI Make time for writing. Put a lot of effort into researching the publication vehicles that you really want to write in so that you are putting yourself in the best possible situation for very good feedback about your writing and potential publication. Those are the two main things. And, not be afraid to write and get feedback. It can be frustrating. The time frame and the turnaround issues can be frustrating but I think they're worthwhile.



**NICOLA So what do you have to say, if anything, about nepotism and gatekeeping within academia?**

LORI I think they're two different things. Maybe nepotism exists – maybe in every industry there would [be] instances of it – but that is not particular to academia. Frankly, it is my experience that in university environments, there's so much attention to accountability and quality assurance that there are systems in place to ensure that nepotism doesn't happen.

In the publishing sense, in terms of nepotism, if you want to think about nepotism in its broadest sense – people who know other people or work with other people, and therefore might favour those people in their reviews, I have never come across it. I've never been in a situation where I felt I received any special treatment in terms of publication because I knew the editor or anyone who may have been a reviewer. There are processes in place for people to declare conflict of interest.

In terms of gatekeeping, the word 'gatekeeping' is not a word that I would use in terms of publication or research grant issues. I think quality is an issue and so I think standards and criteria are well set for funding schemes and journal publications. I think people who are in positions of peer review feel it's important to stick to those standards, address those standards in any kind of feedback that they're giving, or any kind of acceptance or rejection of work that they have had some kind of jurisdiction over. I also think that people are very thoughtful in reviewing standards and criteria in terms of assessing quality. I think that the proliferation of journals over the last few years has meant that people have been able to assess things like scope and criteria because journals seem to set themselves apart. I guess the word 'gatekeeper' is not a word that I would think that I would use myself or think is used in the discourse of publications in academia.

**NICOLA What would you like to say about your observations and the process of getting published within journals, especially prestigious ones?**

LORI It takes a long time – that's my observation of process. If a journal is prestigious, more people are looking to get into those journals. That means that there are lots of submissions to those journals. The editors and peer reviewers for the journal are being asked to do a lot of reviewing and so it takes a lot of time. I think the issue is the turnaround time of getting your work out there. To me, the point of publication is that people understand what you've done and are able to learn from what you've done, but there is a time lag in getting the word out.

I think one of the issues with prestigious journals is partly the amount of submissions that they get and also the need to ensure that they're sticking to that criteria that they set for the journal. If a prestigious journal's criteria starts to slip, then also the prestige of the journal slips. As a reader and potential contributing author, if you stop seeing that kind of quality then you start to question the editorial review board and you start to question the standards.

If the reviewers of the journal take their role seriously, and I think all reviewers do, they take a lot of time to give good feedback and so I think that the other benefit not only is getting a good word out about your research so other people can learn from your research, but getting really good feedback. But the strength of the peer review process is getting that criticism that we talked about before and so if you're going to get a really thoughtful review, that takes time as well.

**NICOLA So what can early career researchers expect from submitting articles to journals for review?**

LORI Well you can expect that you'll get feedback. The feedback will be variable depending on the expertise of the reviewer. Most include at least two reviewers, so the feedback might seem disjointed or there might be discrepancies between the reviews – not every reviewer is going to have the same kind of expertise. So what to expect from submitting to journals is that it's not just about getting the feedback and addressing each point of feedback from a reviewer, it's also having to weigh up the feedback and possibly trying to negotiate between particular competing reviews when discrepancies [occur]. A good editor will help an author through that process. A good editor will take both consistent reviews and discrepant reviews and provide overarching guidance for an author, but that's not always the case. Sometimes editors let the author negotiate between those reviews. The important thing in the process of getting feedback from reviewers is not only in your own thoughtfulness of working with those reviews, not only having that thoughtful processing working within your article, but also being able to explain what you've done and how you've addressed the reviews. That is part of the process and articulating how you've addressed them it is important for an editor. So not just resubmitting a document, actually providing some level of demonstrating your thinking through written [means], these are the reviews I got, this is how I've addressed them and why I have done this with it.



**NICOLA So is there anything you can add about the subjectivity of reviewing with discrepant reviews?**

LORI I don't think it's an issue of subjectivity. I think it's an issue of different expertise. People are on a review board or asked to provide peer review because of their expertise, but everybody's expertise is different in the methodologies they use, in the settings in which they do their research, in the specificity of the discipline area, the theoretical frames which they use. No reviewer is going to have exactly the expertise of the one paper that you [do], because an author has their own expertise so discrepancy isn't surprising because of the range of expertise that reviewers [bring], but I think it's a matter of the author working at negotiating between that discrepancy which might take a bit of work.

**NICOLA What types of things can slow academics down in terms of progress in publications?**

LORI All the other things we have to do besides writing. There's the competing demands of the academic role, particularly when the competing demands are students who are living, breathing bodies who might be in your classroom in the next hour or at your door, not [that there is] any negative thing about them. There's a very positive thing about being a teacher but the demands of teaching are more immediate than the time that we might be able to give to writing, even if writing is a collaborative activity. It's harder to deprioritise students than it is to deprioritise writing. So the time issue is a problem. Then, what we talked about right at the beginning, dealing with the critique and the time it takes and the work that needs to be put in to dealing with critique and feedback in a thoughtful way that's going to make a difference to the paper so I think that can slow someone down. They're probably the biggest issues.

**NICOLA What about distractions and getting involved in extra things like, for instance, I tend not to volunteer for some things because I know they're going to take my time away from writing. Is there anything that you can think of that might be related to that?**

LORI I guess it depends, every academic situation is different. If you are a teaching/research academic, there are lots of different expectations and roles that you need to fill and there are lots of different things that you get out of different activities. So, there are university-wide activities, faculty-wide activities, there's community-based activities. Some might not seem immediately related to your teaching and research. But, they may have flow-on effect in terms of who you meet and what you find out in terms of what might be an interesting research problem that exists or an interesting collaboration that might come out of something that wasn't intended. But you have to find a balance of all those kinds of things and that probably finding the balance is an issue that is part of the negotiating your academic role.



**NICOLA OK, anything else you'd like to add to this topic?**

LORI No, I think we've covered a lot of things.

**NICOLA Great, well thank you very much.**

# 13 Professor Jan Wright

Professor Jan Wright is currently a Professor of Education in the Faculty of Education at the University of Wollongong (UOW) and, for six years, was the Associate Dean (Research) in the Faculty of Education, UOW.

In a career spanning over 30 years, Jan has published widely in the field of physical education and gender, and most recently, in young people's health. Since 1992, Jan has attracted research grant funding of almost AUD$2 million dollars from Australian and New Zealand funding agencies. From 1989, Jan has published more than 40 refereed journal articles, many of them sole-authored. Her recent book publications include the co-editing of *Body Knowledge and Control: Studies in the Sociology of Physical Education and Health* (Evans, Davies and Wright 2004) and *Critical Inquiry and Problem-solving in Physical Education* (Wright, MacDonald and Burrows 2004). She is co-author with Michael Gard of *The Obesity Epidemic: Science, Morality and Ideology* (Gard and Wright 2005) and co-editor of, and writer in the collection, the *Bio-politics of the 'Obesity Epidemic': Governing Bodies* (Wright and Harwood 2009).

Jan is known for her international collaborations (New Zealand, Canada and United Kingdom), along with her extensive research that employs feminist, post-structuralist theories. In this chapter, Jan shares some of her thoughts and experiences about publishing for different genres, the value of a publication, and how one needs to do the required research to ensure publication in certain journals is actually a possibility.

## PROFESSIONAL DIALOGUE

**NICOLA You said that you've got nine publications from your PhD, so can you break them up as to what genre they were?**

JAN Most of them I think were journal articles and the ones on methodology were mostly book chapters, so there's three book chapters and the rest [six] were journal articles.

**NICOLA OK so how did you go about publishing these articles?**

JAN Well, I didn't intend to do it this way, but the way my thesis worked out and the theoretical model that I used meant that I had to understand elements of the social context. One part of the thesis was about the way English bodies – young women's – were constructed in the Olympics, because the argument was, what are the resources that people are drawing on to understand gender? So I had chapters that focused on different topics; they were really discrete. Each of them could easily make a paper or more.

Part of the model was also how did the pedagogy and curriculum of physical education – its genealogy – how did that impact on a physical education lesson, and how did that contribute to the construction of gender? So I did a genealogy of physical education from early on to the 1980s; that became a curriculum studies paper mapping the discourses of physical education. I also did interviews because I wanted to know how students and teachers took up these ideas. That became a paper about how gender was constructed differently by boys and girls but in a kind of complex way etc, that was a paper on complementarity. Then I had papers that came out of the linguistics because that was the data. When I look back at it and what other people do, it wasn't that I just collected a lot of data, I did a lot of analysis of different kinds of sources and each of those enabled me to write for different kinds of journals, for instance, linguistic journals and sport and society type journals. So it was the nature of the thesis. It just absolutely lent itself to writing lots of articles or a book. I think that's an interesting thing because if I'd written a book – one of the examiners, Gunther Kress, said this should be published as a book – I just wasn't in the space to get around to do that. I don't think I would have got those nine articles and I'd have to say I'd rather go for nine articles than one book.

**NICOLA So were there things that you published outside of the PhD that you didn't actually include in the PhD thesis but were part of the study?**

JAN I don't think so, I think that the study was milked. I presented and published a bit on the way, not a lot. I think I published about two papers on the way and presented at conferences and one of the conference papers became a journal article in a linguistic journal.

**NICOLA One area I'd like to explore with you a bit is the idea of why quality journal articles are considered to be more important in terms of publications than a book?**

JAN I think the first is really pragmatic – the number of lines on your CV [curriculum vitae]. I know that there's a European publisher who is approaching European students as well [as those in Australia] because my Swedish student has been approached by Verlag [Editor's note: VDM Verlag is a German publishing house that canvasses for recent theses to publish as books]. She asked me about this because, in Sweden, the university makes about 80 copies of your thesis and they keep some and they sell the rest, so that was a question about whether it had already been published or not. So there is a kind of tradition in Europe of having a book-like monograph, particularly in the Scandinavian countries, and it's a little book. It's got a lovely cover on it and all those sorts of things. But that's changing now, so that's going to be different. They [academics] have to publish, so I don't know whether Verlag's kind of picking up on that and just extending that into a commercial kind of publishing thing. So in that context you don't have to do much to your thesis, but in the context in which [a colleague] and I and others publish, with Routledge for instance, you have to do a lot to your thesis – they don't publish theses. One exception might be Peter Lang Publishing. A lot of people have published their thesis through Peter Lang but you have to do a lot of work. First of all it has to be accepted and they usually accept theoretically robust theses, but again you have to do all the work on it, like you have to do the editing. They don't ask you to do the changes that Routledge would ask you to do which would be 'make this into something that looks like all the other books we published' and that's not like a thesis. So at that time for me, that's what it would have meant to get the thesis published as a book. I would have had to sit down and make it into a book and it was too much. One journal article at a time was a much more straightforward way to go. Also, to get the findings of the thesis out there much more quickly.



**NICOLA The journal articles?**

JAN Yeah, the journal articles get it out there more quickly, but a book can make your name. If the books are picked up, that's the difference I think between having a publisher who will really actively market your book and put it into the commercial arena and take it to conferences and all those sorts of things. Then you know people will read it. They [the publishers] will pick it up and they will make sure that it is marketable, like it has the right title and all those sorts of things and gets put up for awards. I'm not sure whether Verlag is going to do that, I just don't know. I think it's going to be up to academics themselves to market it and they're just hoping that by putting it on the web, people will pick the name up using key words and then want the book because I'm assuming they'll be reasonably priced. So I don't know, I think Verlag is the space to watch because they're certainly canvassing anyone that seems to have an interesting thesis.

**NICOLA Yes, or just anyone.**

JAN Yes I know, I wonder whether they pick up on a database in the universities or something or they pick up on graduations and they just send invitations. I don't know if they even read the abstracts or summaries. I did meet a Verlag person once. They wanted us to write a book on something else and I'd be really interested to ask them because I think it's a really interesting question. It will shift thinking and it might not be a good thing. It might mean that people think I've published out of this, I've published my thesis so therefore I can't write anything out of it and that's not true. I think a book is really different from a journal. I think doing both if you've got the energy is good.



**NICOLA Can you talk a bit more about the differences in genre between the thesis and the journal article?**

JAN One of the things is your [thesis] chapters are usually much longer than a journal article. In the journal article you have to use a lot of your words up actually writing about your purpose and methodology before you can get to what was actually in the chapter so I think it's a risk to take a chapter and just think, 'I'll just sort of cut bits here and there and send a chapter off.' I think a journal article is different. A journal article requires an angle, it requires a location within a literature, particularly updated literature that's probably more recent than your thesis and it certainly has to have an introduction that's different from what you usually find as an introduction to a thesis chapter. It has to have a literature and it depends on the nature and that's what was so good about my thesis chapters. Every chapter had discrete literature, because in my thesis, each chapter had a literature review, had a methodology and it had what I did.

**NICOLA That was conducive to ...?**

JAN It was very conducive to publish, and I think that's the difference between most people's chapters is that their method and their literature review is at the front end of the book and then there's the methodology and then there's some findings. But there might be chapters that have different kinds of angles and each of those angles could make a very nice journal article. There might be something about the context of the schools and the nature of the schools or the nature of the people and then there might be thematic stuff in another chapter. That's fine and they make good journal articles but they have to have a front end which means you have to bring some of the front end from the rest of your thesis and then you're way over words so then you have to kind of distance yourself from it. You have to think, what is it that I could say and could I have two journal articles? That's the thing, say you have a lot of sections to a chapter and you've got a lot of angles, you know, different sorts of things that you're trying to say, well often just one of those angles will make a good journal article.



**NICOLA We spoke last week about the difficulties of publishing during your thesis and how that it seems to be more promoted and more beneficial if you can do that, so what is your opinion on that?**

JAN I think it's so tough <laughing>. I think if you're full time you should be thinking about how you could publish. I think if you start thinking about it from the beginning, like [a doctoral student], she did six interviews for her pilot and I think if she finds an angle out of those and uses theory in a more illustrative way and gets a paper out of it, that would be a good result from her first year. It means she has to be really on top of the theory because she's trying to illustrate theory rather than rely so heavily on her findings because she's only got a small number of interviews. I think it's hard because I think journals don't like work in progress. I think literature review articles are a possibility but I think that if people are going to start publishing more and more out of qualitative research, all they'll have to publish is their literature review after the first year. You have to be very, very good at that and you have to again be saying, 'How do I critique this literature?', so it's not like, 'Here's the literature, look, I did a data base search and here it all is.' You have to be able to show that you're a scholar in relation to that and that you've got something new to say and to contribute to knowledge because otherwise no one will publish it.

I think that's the danger now. The place is going to be bombarded by not very good literature reviews and they'll just get knocked back and doctoral students will feel bad and all those sorts of things. I think doing qualitative research in that whole notion of emerging insight is hugely difficult to do. I think though by the end of the second year, if you were full time, you should be able to write something that will be part of your thesis. I think that's the thing that you have to think about. Whatever you write shouldn't be that extra bit outside the thesis if you haven't got the time to do that, it should be something that you can put into your thesis and it will enable you to do the analysis that you need to do for your thesis. I mean the thing with education is that so many of our postdoctoral students are also academics and they have to publish, and you know they can't afford to wait. That's like [another doctoral student] we talked about – he will do his thesis by publication. They've been doing it in biomechanics forever and in science so it's not that it's not ever been acceptable but it's been unusual in education and the social sciences. But he's an academic, he has to have publications and also he has so much data that when we planned the chapters we said, 'Plan the chapters as articles' and now we've become even more specific about that. So you could still do a thesis and we could think of the chapters as being potential journal articles. But we thought the better way to go was for them to be journal articles and to go for the thesis by publication so that's what he's going to do.



**NICOLA What were some difficulties you faced in publishing your PhD?**

JAN Oh well, I think it was that first article. I sent it off to the most prestigious journal at the time, an American journal in physical education. I'm pretty much the first person to do post-structuralist work in PE [physical education], almost internationally, and I didn't want to compromise. I thought it was a really good paper and I liked it and it was readable and all those sorts of things and I sent it there. I don't think they rejected it outright. I wish I'd kept the comments but my sense was that they wanted a rewrite and they wanted all these things which were to fit it to their genre which was the usual genre which they wanted a methodology and they wanted a literature review. I can't remember what else they said because I know what they've said about more recent ones and I know it's part of their thinking. I don't think it was even that big a deal but I was also teaching a lot and I just couldn't contemplate it. So I went to my [PhD] supervisor and said, 'I can't do this.' I said, 'They want me to do it in this scientific mode and I just can't face it', so I said, 'If you help me with it we'll go joint author.' He said yes. I can't remember what he did, but he didn't do very much, but what he did do was enable me to come back into it and to do it in the way they wanted me to do, which was with literature review, methodology, findings and not too much extrapolation from the findings. [This journal doesn't] like you to theorise from the findings, they don't like you going too far – that's the feedback I've gotten from more recent papers. So in the end I don't think he did very much. We talked about it, he probably told me just do this and do that and put a heading in here and organise it like this. I don't think there were huge changes to it in the end and it did get published. But that first, 'Oh I don't even know how to begin here, I don't even want to know' was really hard, so it was great having someone who helped me get over that. I guess from then on, I began to understand that revisions were feedback <laughing> and they weren't personal attacks. Because I knew the paradigm that they were working from and I was thinking, 'Why do I have to fit into their paradigm, can't they accept something new?' you know, all those sorts of things, so that was all my huffing and puffing around the place, so I needed someone to help me get past that.

**NICOLA What was a memorable experience you had as an early career academic?**

JAN I shouldn't think too hard about this because then you get flooded but I think for me it was moving to linguistics and being part of the linguistics community and having people like Jim Martin say, 'You're pretty intelligent for a physical education person aren't you?' <laughing>. So, just going to linguistics conferences and being part of the social semiotics group which was Jim Martin, Michael Halliday and Terry Threadgold, who was my other supervisor was great. Just being amongst those people and the talk about theory, and the excitement about analytical frameworks using linguistics was great. Having those tools and being able to bring that back into physical education was memorable. It did make me a very, very big frog in a very, very small pond, <laughing> globally, let's say, but the experience of being involved with the linguistics people and systemic functioning was fantastic.



**NICOLA So that really sort of boosted you and got you excited?**

JAN Oh excited, hugely excited, I still love linguistics. I just love it because it's a tool. It gives you a handle when in so much qualitative analysis you're kind of thrashing around. It gives you a really good way of looking at language and you've got a framework there to understand what's going on in the text.

**NICOLA Can you explain an experience in your career that was really a surprise or a good fortune that sort of helped you along the way?**

JAN When I said to my colleagues, 'I want to know how gender is constructed in these lessons and nobody's using sexist language <laughing>, so what am I going to do? I think something's going on.' They said, 'Well you've got to do linguistics, you've got to look at the language more closely because it's not the words.' So having some colleagues saying I had to do this was the biggest, most amazing thing that happened.

**NICOLA Have you an anecdote you can share about a frustrating experience about publishing in a journal?**

JAN You hear stories about some journals losing your paper or the editor changes and they just don't know where it's gone and you follow up and then they say it hasn't been reviewed. I've experienced those kinds of frustrations particularly with one paper. The other frustrations were trying to publish and to make a difference in physical education when you're batting your head against paradigms even as the field of physical education research moves more to qualitative research. It wasn't that they weren't doing qualitative research, it was that they were very atheoretical and even in recent times with those sorts of journals, they want detail from your qualitative data but they don't want you to theorise from it. You can't because you're going beyond the data and that's the comment you receive. In that case [another colleague] and I published in that type of journal keeping it contained to the data, and then for another journal, we theorised it and published it, so then we could say the things that we really wanted to say about what we thought was going on and get into the theory. So there has been a constant sort of frustration. I don't try and publish in certain journals now that other journals have been set up and are doing gender work or doing work that is more theoretically sophisticated.



**NICOLA What advice would you give to early career researchers?**

JAN You know, I read that question earlier and I was thinking, one of the ways of getting things going and published is to do an edited collection with someone else, usually someone who has a bit of reputation because if you're going through Routledge for instance, they want to know who the editors are and what is the basis. Chapters are one of the ways to get published without some of those other frustrations. I wouldn't stack an edited collection with a whole lot of your own papers but bringing really interesting people in is a way of networking as well, canvassing who's writing something of interest in the field. It is again a way of getting your name out there, if the book gets taken up, you may be the editor and you will have some papers in it but it's sort of one way of networking and also getting a line on the CV. If you're in the bureaucracy and publications don't matter and you're not trying to build a career in that way, well then lines on your CV don't matter. But if you are in the academy, lines on your CV do matter and then the quality of those lines matters. So I would think going for refereed publications in conference collections to begin with may be the quickest way of getting something on your CV. They are counted at the moment with DEST [Department of Education, Science and Training, points from which universities are funded] and as long as they're reasonably credible, I think you should start to build a CV that way. Develop those into journal articles or develop other angles into journal articles. Journal articles sometimes take two years to get published so you have to be looking at the short and the long term. The short term is to get something on your CV that's credible and sensible, so if they are conference papers, they should be refereed. Aim to have a journal article in a really top journal but meanwhile keep developing journal articles for ones that have a faster turnover and that are still credible. I think in your early stages of a career it's about getting published and that's why I sort of wonder about devoting all the time to a book if you're not publishing something else at the same time.

And I would say go to conferences. You have to present because otherwise people won't know who you are, and they won't respond to your papers and it's one way of getting feedback on your ideas. Also, people give you ideas about what's the latest and those sorts of things and it's certainly about networking. If you have a supervisor or anyone else that can introduce you to people, or you can join Special Interest Groups (SIGs) and find collections of people to associate yourself with, you can build networks.



**NICOLA What would you like to say about your observations about the process of getting published within journals, especially prestigious ones?**

JAN I think you should do a bit of homework first. I think that's really important. Many fairly prestigious journals, well this is my experience anyway, some of them have a particular philosophical position or paradigmatic position, you want to know whether you've got a chance of getting published. I don't need to give you a specific example but there was a journal that was a really high journal in the whole sociology of health field. I submitted an article and got feedback. The first lot of feedback was just obviously from someone who didn't know much about and didn't like [Michel] Foucault and I enjoyed myself in responding to that. The other person was more an ethnographer and wanted more detail, wanted it more ethnographic. When you respond to revisions you don't have to make every revision but you have to respond to every suggestion for a revision, but you don't have to make all of them. You should talk to other people before you decide you won't make them, but you should also say why you're not going to make it. So for this example, I responded and said what I thought. I carefully worded it, I drafted and redrafted and redrafted. I didn't want to put anyone off side and then I sent it back and asked for that assessor not to assess it again. The second time round it was still rejected and it was partly because what they wanted was a more substantial explanation of the ethnographic aspects of it and it wasn't a pure or classical ethnography. I can't remember what the other review was but it wasn't quite so pointed which made it harder to deal with. But I think I was also disappointed because I did my homework, I tried to locate it in relation to the debates in the journal but it still got rejected. But we revised it and sent it off to [Journal A], and it got published. So I think you have to do your homework so you don't put all of your energies into something where your chances of getting rejected are high.

You have to also expect these days that you could have a two-year turnaround on submitted journal articles, but some journals are faster than others. I'm not sure about this but ones that have the whole process online, to me it's a bit of a signal that they are organised. It's partly because I've had another experience with two journals in the sociology of sport, one which is online and one which isn't. The one that is not online is [very slow and seems unorganised] – I know from one of our students – she's just had so much trouble. They couldn't find the paper, we had to ring you know. Both supervisors had to bring in heavy guns because we also know the person and say, 'Excuse me, this isn't acceptable' and we almost went to the subeditors, so that seemed to me things aren't organised there, whereas, with the other journal, you know where your article is because they use electronic tracking. So you can actually track your article, you feel like it's there and that you know where it is, it's not in somebody's cardboard box, so I think that's often a useful signal. Things to consider include whether people know about the typical length of the turnaround, is the editor really good, what kind of feedback do you get, you know, what are you likely to get if you send your journal article there? Ask people about the editorial board and what the editor is like, that's useful information.

I'd also ensure that you have somebody else, a supervisor or somebody else, read your journal article before you send it off because there's nothing that will get up the nose of reviewers more than having a half-baked, poorly presented, very early stage kind of journal article, because they don't see themselves as supervisors, you know. As a reviewer myself, I often want to write back and say, 'Where is your supervisor? They should have given more assistance.' Sometimes as a reviewer, you just feel like that's what you're doing, you're doing the role of a supervisor. So you should only send polished papers off that have been read by at least one or two other more experienced people to get feedback beforehand. That will also be faster. You don't want more and more delays because you have to make two lots of revisions as well.

**NICOLA So what can early career researchers expect from submitting articles to journals for review?**

JAN Well it depends on the article. In Sweden, you have to put that you're a doctoral student so you can expect a rejection <laughing>. I think you should submit journal articles which look like a polished contribution to knowledge. Even if they are work in progress, they shouldn't look like work in progress.

Often people who are doing PhDs are at the cutting edge because they've got the time to be reading, they should have been reading the latest stuff, they've got fresh data and they should have something to say, but they need to do their homework about the genre and nature of the journal and all those sorts of things. I think you should expect feedback, I mean I think everyone should. I think there would be few people who don't get some feedback and I think sometimes they should be ready for feedback that might be quite substantial in terms of changes. They shouldn't then put it in a cupboard, you know. The delays between, like I know when you [Nicola] did it [a revision], you got back to them really quickly. That's what you should do and a lot of journals will say you have to send it back within this amount of time if you want this published, which is good, because that means they're going to publish it. You should make every effort to do that and if it means going and asking for help or even bringing someone else on to the paper to get that done then you should do it, but don't put it at the bottom of the cupboard because you don't want to look at it anymore, it's just part of the process.



**NICOLA So rejection is normal?**

JAN No, rejection's not normal. I only reject papers that are really bad. Major revisions means there's something interesting here but it probably needs a pretty big rewrite and I would try and be as specific as I can. If people ask you for major revisions they usually tell you what they want and it's just like you've been through a thesis process. If you had to do revision to that, it's the same, you read through it, talk through it with someone else and you decide if this is going to enhance the paper or if it's really something that you're just going to be knocking your head against and it's a paradigmatic thing [clash]. If they want you to change the paper in ways you don't feel comfortable with, then it's not necessarily a rejection of your paper, it's a rejection of the paper from that journal and you might think of sending it somewhere else but still taking into account the feedback. It's useless to send the article to another journal if some of the feedback is along the lines of, 'I really didn't understand where you were going' or, 'The literature review was a bit dated' or you know, there's some feedback that will help you enhance it before sending it off to another journal. There's other feedback that you just think well they're just coming from a different place.

I think the other thing is, editors do not moderate. It's very rare and people have to realise that. It's like the ethics committee, it's a collection of responses so sometimes responses will be contradictory, so it's no use throwing up your hands and saying, 'Oh they're all saying different things.' You have to work out which works in your favour in a way, because you can point out that the reviews are contradictory and you are in agreement with this, this but not that, but because the editors don't have time to moderate, they often don't read the reviewers' reports (especially the electronic versions). They just send them to you, and that's something you've got to understand. I think that means you have to moderate and that means that you have to decide, you know, as a scholar whether these are reasonable or not, and whether the suggested revisions enhance your paper or whether they change what you wanted to say. You have to make decisions about these things and I think it's useful to make decisions with the assistance of your supervisor or your colleagues, at least in those early papers.

**NICOLA Do you have anything to say about nepotism and gatekeeping in academia?**



JAN Actually, there was a really good paper given by Patti Lather. I don't know if she wrote it up. It was a symposium at AERA [American Educational Research Association conference] and a lot of the debate was about whether reviewers' names should be on reviews or not and that was about nepotism and gatekeeping.

I'm just trying to work through this. In America, you have big editorial boards and those members are obviously supervisors of a whole lot of students so their aim is to get them published. If you look at [Journal B], there's reams of the same people being published, and I think if you traced them to who the editorial board was at the time, I think there'd be a bit of a relationship. But I think there's also the other side of it which is why you go to conferences – that's why you ask your supervisor to introduce you to people, that's why you choose your examiners carefully. I think in the assessment process, if you're in a small field, people will certainly identify it. I mean you can't imagine that you won't be identified [as a reviewer] and that shouldn't be a problem but sometimes it really is helpful because people might feel well disposed. For instance, they may have seen you present at a conference and they thought the paper was interesting, they think it needs a bit more work, so you get good feedback and they're trying to get you on your way. So I think those sorts of things happen.

It's hard for me to say because I'm one of the gatekeepers or the nepotists you know, in a sense. I try and foster people like when I go to Scandinavia, there's a lot of people there who are supposed to write in English so with my friend H, I'll say to J [editor of journal], 'Look, I know there's a lot of people that are writing from Scandinavia and they're trying to get published. If you want me to work with their papers I'll do that.' I worked with H's paper to get it past the 'this is incomprehensible because it's not in English sort of stage' and I think, with [Journal C], it's almost the opposite. It has to be really bad to not get positive and helpful feedback. How you interpret that is a different thing but it [the journal] tries to be really inclusive. I think other journals are clearly more hardnosed and I think the ones that are trying to demonstrate their quality I suppose or hold a particular position at the top of the ISI[1] are probably much more difficult to get into. I think you have to make decisions about whether, certainly at the beginning of your career, you actually wouldn't want to take them on unless you've got something hugely theoretically or amazing to say and I wouldn't take an American journal as your first step [if you are Australian] unless you're working within a more positivist framework as a general [rule] <laughing>.

**NICOLA So anything else to add to finish off?**

JAN There are a lot of journals out there now. The other thing I would say is that I wouldn't buy into the rhetoric in some faculties – I don't mean here – which could actually prevent you from publishing at all because you think you have to be in the most high-quality top ISI journal. I think that kind of rhetoric for early career researchers can just stop them from publishing.



**NICOLA Mmm, it's just too much.**

JAN It's just too hard and I think especially in education, there are good reasons why you might publish in particular places because you're trying to reach a readership. You can also find problems with those journal bandings. If you want another source, if it's not a psych[ology] journal with a top ISI impact factor, you may actually be able to use those bandings to say, well, at least from this point of view, this is regarded as a high-quality journal, this is an international journal it reaches da, da, da. I think you have to be a bit careful in your early career, unless you can write the article really quickly, writing for professional refereed journals like the [Journal C]. Its problem is its name but it is a refereed journal and it does report research and it does speak to a professional community as well as to the academic community. And you can get a quick turnaround, so it would be worth publishing in that journal. If you've got journals that are professional journals, that are refereed, and they have a reasonably quick turnaround, sure they probably want a fairly short article, it won't replace the kind of highly esteemed journal publication, but publishing in it will build your CV and also get your name out there. Having something published makes you feel good about it; it's good to see yourself

1 Now known as Thomson Reuters Web of Knowledge.

in print. I think that's really important. When you talk about buzzes, seeing yourself in print is a huge buzz.

**NICOLA OK, well that's a great place to end.**

# 14 Professor Wilma Vialle

A former high school teacher of English, speech and drama, Professor Wilma Vialle lectures in educational psychology and gifted education in the Faculty of Education at the University of Wollongong. Two of Wilma's best-known publications, both with Judy Perry, are *Teaching through the Eight Intelligences* (Vialle and Perry 2002) and *Nurturing Multiple Intelligences in the Australian Classroom* (Vialle and Perry 1995).

Her latest book, written with Professor Karen Rogers, is entitled *Educating the Gifted Learner* (Vialle and Rogers 2009). Alongside 11 books, Wilma has published almost 20 book chapters and 30 refereed journal articles. She is a popular, international keynote speaker. Wilma has supervised more than 20 higher degree students to completion. She led the Faculty of Education's successful AUD$2.6 million tender for the School Counsellor Training Program from the Department of Education and Training in New South Wales (2008–2011). Wilma has attracted over AUD$600,000 in research grants from 1995–2011, and USD$140,000 for her work in Florida (USA) in the early 1990s. She is the co-editor of the *Australasian Journal of Gifted Education*. Wilma is working closely with Professor Sara Dolnicar (interviewed in Chapter 15) on an Australian Learning and Teaching Council project (2010–2012) that seeks to mentor early career academics.

In this chapter, Wilma gives specific insight into the field of specialisation, and the difficulties that this can impose. She also highlights some of the difficulties associated with joint authorship.

## PROFESSIONAL DIALOGUE

**NICOLA Wilma, when and where did you receive your PhD?**

WILMA OK, I received it in December in 1991 and it was at the University of South Florida in Tampa, Florida.

**NICOLA Yes, what made you go to Florida?**

WILMA Well, I had no intention of doing a PhD. That was one of the interesting things. I was teaching in Tasmania and doing my Masters degree part time. The final component of that was a thesis in which I looked at gifted kids in the school in which I was working. There was nobody at the University of Tasmania who had any expertise in that area. So I basically gained my expertise from reading books and journal articles and so on. So when I finished that thesis I didn't think I was at the end of something, I actually felt as if I was at the beginning of something. So I thought what I wanted to do was have more experience in the gifted field and more direction. I went over to the United States simply because most of what I'd been reading came out of the United States so it seemed like a logical thing to do. This was pre-email days, so I sent letters through the mail <laughing> to a number of universities asking [about] their programs in gifted education and I only got seven replies. From those there were only two that looked as if they had a program that would enable me to specialise in gifted education and one was [Columbia] Teachers College in New York and the other one was the University of South Florida in Tampa, Florida. Because I came from a fairly cold place I just thought going to a hot place would be [good], and so it was as accidental as that.

When I first arrived there I got talking to the person who [wa]s in charge of the whole program – she was only there for two days in the entire summer that I was there – but I was able to have a meeting with her on the first day and she took my Masters thesis home with her and read it overnight and then caught up with me the next day. She said, 'Look, if you know this much, you're wasting your time' because, I was just [going to do] another Masters Degree. She said, 'Why don't you do a doctorate?' I said, 'Well because I've only got money for one year', and she said to me, 'Oh there's always money' and I said 'OK'. It was as simple as that, so I transferred to the doctoral program and there was always money and I came home without any debt at all.

**NICOLA Oh great.**

WILMA So it was really good. I did it in fairly quick time. From the day I arrived in the US until the day I successfully defended my PhD was only two and a half years.

**NICOLA Oh wow.**

WILMA So I worked fairly hard.

**NICOLA So did you do much course work?**

WILMA Yeah, I basically did the thesis component in one year and I radically accelerated. Most people were taking three subjects as a full-time student. I was taking five and so on <laughing>.

**NICOLA Right, OK, so how many publications did you get out of your PhD?**



WILMA In terms of journal articles, probably only a couple but [I] also had a couple of published conference papers in selected proceedings.

**NICOLA So how did you divide up your thesis to put the publications together?**

WILMA It was mainly around audience, so that was the main consideration. I probably need to fill that in by saying what my thesis was about, so my interest was gifted ed[ucation] and I was trying to look at alternative means of identifying gifted kids who came from non-mainstream groups because they were seriously underrepresented in gifted programs. This [wa]s my observation from looking at programs in the US. In Tasmania, we didn't really have any [programs] anyway. So I started looking at multiple intelligences theory as a kind of lens to look at children more broadly than IQ tests. I ended up doing intensive case studies of five African-American preschoolers, which was interesting – being a trained high school teacher to turn around and do your research with three- to five-year-olds. I learnt a lot and gained a lot of respect for early childhood teachers at the same time.

So one of the obvious audiences to me when I got back was looking at special needs education, so I looked at how multiple intelligences theory could be used as a means of identifying kids who didn't show up on IQ tests, so looking at cultural difference. So I took that kind of [approach that] this might be a means of identifying children from minority cultural groups and as I went on and did other work, [I] came to look at low socioeconomic-statuses (SESs) as well and it grew into deaf kids as [a] specific cultural group and so on. So there were a whole range of things that spun off from that in that kind of gifted ed. Then the other audience was special education more generally, and thinking about kids that might have disabilities. Rather than taking a deficit approach to children with problems, [let's] think about their strengths and can we help remediate their weak areas by drawing on their strength areas. So that was another audience, so that was another paper there. Then I did a presentation here about my research and [a colleague] said to me, 'Oh you know you should write this up for an early childhood journal and this one would be really good so why don't you do it', so then I wrote it from the perspective of looking at observation, how you go about observing early childhood and sort of getting some sense of children. So that's how it played out thinking about the same material but from the point of view of different audiences.

**NICOLA OK, great, so what were some difficulties you faced in publishing from your PhD?**



WILMA Knowing where to publish and what. Once you've done the first one and then sort of where do you go from there ... haven't you already written it all and so on, that was difficult. I guess in some senses I relied very heavily on people giving me clues such as [a colleague] saying, 'Oh why don't you focus on the early childhood?' or other colleagues saying, 'Look there's this special ed conference coming up, why don't you do something for that?'

I came into this position at the University of Wollongong with no colleagues in my content area, I came in to do ed[ucation] psych[ology] and basically the two people I worked with were non-publishers, they did no research whatsoever. At that time there was nobody interested in gifted ed at all here and so I was very much alone, a lone person and didn't really know how to go about things. I was a brand new academic so I wasn't an academic who did a PhD, I was a teacher who did a PhD and then because I went back to Tasmania and had a PhD, people asked me to do some part-time teaching at the university and I found I really enjoyed working with adults in that way. So it was only when I got a full-time position here that I suddenly realised, 'Gosh, I'd better do something about publishing.' In my interview they said, 'Well, you have a PhD but you don't have any publications, what's that about <laughing>?' As a teacher you don't need to publish, so I knew I had to get up to speed very quickly and that was frustrating not really knowing where to direct things.

**NICOLA Can you talk more about the difficulty you faced with being alone and trying to work through things by yourself?**

WILMA That's what it basically comes down to because you've got nobody. I had every research group here come to talk to me about my research and would I fit in with their group. Most of them didn't want to know about me because they couldn't see how I could fit in. One of the research groups sort of took me on and the person who headed that up was very helpful in the sense of saying, 'You should apply for a university small grant, you should apply for this, you should do that', so giving me that kind of direction. But the frustration came around not really having anybody to talk to about the discipline knowledge. [I was thinking] so I've done this PhD but how do I take the next step and what should that step look like? So it's those kinds of frustrations. I write pretty well, but having someone that could say, 'Well, because your area is [such and such] and you're interested in these kinds of things, these are the kinds of journals you should be shooting for', or even how to write for particular journals. It was not really having anybody [to] be able to talk to you about those things because they don't know how it applies in your discipline/area.



**NICOLA What is a memorable experience you had as an early career academic?**

WILMA I think one of the things that the leader of the research group said to me was, 'Is there anything else you did in your degree that you could write about?' For a kind of history of ed class, I'd done a really good reanalysis of some historical work of a key figure in gifted ed. So I dragged that out and thought, 'Well, where could this go and what could I do with it?' I tell you that would be the most chewed over <laughing> piece of work. I rewrote the research that I'd done for probably the top international journal in gifted ed, but I was not at all confident about how it w[ould] go before I submitted it. I remember having that perfectionist trait in me and not wanting to let it go. I actually sent an email around to the faculty saying, 'Look I know nobody else is in my area but I've written this article. Would anybody be willing to read it for me and give me some feedback?' A couple of people did and they were really simple things, like I had written it as an essay without a single heading in the entire thing, so that was just one piece of feedback that somebody gave me. Anyway, that was probably the only real advice I got from other people other than, 'Oh yes it's interesting.' So it was all ready to go but still not able to let it go. I was riding on a train up to Sydney one time and I was reading it for the nine hundredth time. Suddenly I realised that the very first opening sentence of the thing made no sense whatsoever, it was just fluff. So I changed that and sent it off and it was published without any changes needed.

I guess what made it memorable for me – thinking it was just this little trivial kind of paper – was when one of the top names in gifted ed then cited my paper and so it was like, wow <laughing>. This really important person whose work I had cited, I hadn't met her, and she was just such a big name, actually used something that I wrote. I got a report back later on that she had said that the article was very influential in how she looked at a whole range of things, so that was for me a memorable experience in a lot of ways. Sometimes you can just agonise too much. I spent so much time on that paper and yes, it was then published without needing any changes, but the reality is you don't need to agonise that much over things. You can use the feedback that you get from journals to rejig things and I think that that's one of the mistakes early academics make is that they spend too long trying to perfect something.

**NICOLA So could you talk about how rare it is to get a journal article accepted without changes?**

WILMA That's the one and only time <laughing>. I've had things come back three times to me that need this change or need that change or whatever. Even after you think you've addressed the things that they've asked for, it still comes back again. It can be very frustrating too because you can get feedback that says you need to change a lot of this to this, and then you send it back and there may have been some delay in sending it back, and they might have a new editor and the new editor thinks, 'Oh, I'll just send it out again' and then you get more feedback that [causes] you [to] go back to where you started so, it can be a tortuous process.



The more highly regarded the journal is, the more submissions they will receive, the more time they take to get back to you, the more likelihood that there is a change of editor, which means that there can be further delays because they send it back out again rather than going on what the previous editor had decided. You get all of these little games they play, so yes, it's very, very difficult to get things published, but nothing's ever lost. Even after I've had things that have been rejected, I've sent them somewhere else and they get accepted and that's fine, but I've had things that have just been rejected and then what I've done is I've just used chunks of that for other writing. Nothing's ever really wasted at the end of the day.

**NICOLA That's encouraging <laughing>. Have you an anecdote you can share about a frustrating experience about publishing in a journal?**

WILMA A particular paper that was done with a couple of colleagues ... was sent to a journal. It took a long time, something like eight months, to come back. There were a number of reviews and it took me a couple of months to address all of the things but I rewrote it basically and resent it and it was the same deal. There had been a change in editor and a change in policy. It went back out again and then there was another set of changes that needed to be made. In the meantime, there had been some personal issues with one of the co-authors and myself and it was one of those deals where the three of us all agreed to take the lead on one paper each, and put the others' names on basically. I was the only one who actually did it. At the end of the day, having rewritten this article twice, I decided not to do the final change because if I put that article out in any form whatsoever, I would have to put the colleague's name on it and it seemed to me that this person didn't hold up their end of the bargain. So that was a frustrating experience because I felt as if I had invested a lot of time and energy into this particular article and then it went nowhere. Later I used one of the examples – it was my example, so there was no way it was from the collected, shared data, it was another thing that I had put in from my data – so I used that part of it but the rest of it I just had to throw away.



The other thing is another frustration, it's not the most frustrating, but it is frustrating for me, is that is my [family] name starts with the letter V and sometimes when you're working in groups and it's been equal share it's often, 'Well, how do we decide what order to put the names in?' Quite often the decision is, 'We'll do it alphabetically' and I'm always last. I've been on a number of group papers where I have put in as much work as anybody else but I've been third or fourth or fifth author on the paper because of my <laughing> [surname]. I've thought about changing my name by deed poll to put AA in front of the Vialle so have my name Aavialle <laughing>.

So I think you need to negotiate those kinds of things in teams when there are multiple papers coming out of a project. That's the advice that I give young academics that I supervise is to say, 'Negotiate upfront which articles you will take the lead on so that you can get that first [authorship].'

**NICOLA So leading on from that what advice would you give to early career researchers?**

WILMA OK, yes, you've got to develop thick skin and that's one of the hardest things when you're an expert on something. When you've done a PhD, you are the expert in that particular area and the hardest thing is to put yourself out there for your peers to judge. What reviewers will say can be really hurtful and they will say them for all sorts of reasons. One reason is that you haven't cited them and they think they're the expert and so they will just completely dismiss your work as being completely irrelevant. Or you've taken the wrong tack because you've trodden on somebody's hallowed ground. Therefore, look at the journal carefully, look at quite a few issues, who publishes in that journal, and who's publishing in a similar field to you in that journal, who's on the editorial board, do they publish in a similar area? If they do, make darn well sure that you're citing them in a positive way in your work because it's likely to go to them to be reviewed. So that's an important element, you've got to know your field.

I have a PhD student who's trying to publish out of her honours at the moment and it's basically been rejected. But I've just read the rejection and it's really obvious that the journal is more focused towards quantitative research because of the nature of the feedback that she's been given (and there's only one reviewer). The kinds of things that they're saying are totally irrelevant to a qualitative piece of research so clearly what this student hasn't done is she hasn't looked closely enough at what the journal is publishing. Because, if it's predominantly quantitative then the reviewers are probably predominantly quantitative in their approach, and so getting something qualitative published in a journal that is predominantly quantitative means that you have to go that extra step in terms of demonstrating the rigour of your method and being very conservative in terms of the implications of it. You have to be careful about those kinds of things. So that's the one thing, you need to really do your homework, you just don't go for, 'Oh that's an A journal or that's the big one in this field so that's the one I'm shooting for.' But as I say, I think if you're trying to get up to speed you need multiple strategies, so you need to be working on getting that A-journal publication, but be prepared that that process might take a couple of years and because it does take a couple of years and there is that point of time, shoot for some easier publications as well. In other words, don't put all of your eggs into the basket of getting that article in *Nature* [Editor note: top-ranked science journal]. If you can get *Nature,* well, that's wonderful or whatever the equivalent is in the field, but in the meantime, do the other things as well.

The other thing is turn over your conference papers. Even if they do have some kind of publication of [their conference proceedings], conferences will often be non-refereed and you retain the copyright. So you should use the feedback that you might have got at the session and turn those papers into journal articles as well. So try to maximise the various locations. With tweaking, rewriting something for a different audience so you've got a different slant on it – but you're basically using the same data source – again helps you to spread yourself out across things.

**NICOLA Great, do you have anything to say about nepotism and gatekeeping in academia?**

WILMA It happens, there's no doubt about it and that's why alignment is a good idea, so networking. It's not even that it's deliberate nepotism but, you know, if you happen to meet somebody at a conference and you've got good ideas, when they're under the gun and they need something in a hurry they'll think, 'Oh yes, that person I met at that conference or whatever, she had some interesting things to say, I'll just shoot her an email.' You might pick up an edited book with chapters from a number of people and you think, 'Well, I could have contributed a chapter to this, I know a lot about this kind of stuff' but you don't know the editor. The editor has asked their friends. It's very rare that a book editor shoots something out to the entire population and says, 'Do you want to submit a chapter on this?' They don't, they ask their friends, they ask their network of people that they've met at the last conference or, you know, they get talking about it with others, and 'We should put a book together on this' happens. Making those kinds of networks helps get through that.



To some extent I know that if there were particular people who were editing particular journals, I would be wasting my time sending my stuff there because they hate me. Therefore, they wouldn't send it out for review. They would just say it's been rejected because they have a different mindset and they see you as a threat. So that kind of thing happens. Fortunately, I think that that is the minority, and it might be just my experience, but I think a lot of people are willing to see beyond it.

But if you look beyond research to academic careers generally, there's a lot of nepotism, favouritism, in crowd, out crowd, and so on, and it's hard if you've got strong opinions and you believe in expressing these strong opinions. It's very hard not to offend somebody along the way. You can't be well liked by everybody. Some people actually thrive on that, you know, creating trouble. Some people just like to be controversial and like the thrill of the debate or the argument, whereas other people need that kind of agreement.

**NICOLA OK, so have you got anything you can add to what you've already said about the process of getting published within journals, especially prestigious ones?**

WILMA I think it's a building thing. These prestigious journals tend to be very broad ranging journals and that's why they're prestigious because they have a wide audience and, therefore, they have more impact factor because that's the numbers game. When people are looking for journals that have higher impact factors – and that's how you're going to increase under Excellence in Research Australia (ERA) and schemes like that – that are putting so much emphasis on high-impact journals because it comes down to a metric all the time.

Well, if I'm doing research in gifted ed, that's got to be my first [priority]. But if I want to be in a high-impact journal, it's not going to be in a gifted journal, so my problem is that the umbrella, which is education and psychology, is dominated by quantitative research. So for me to get published in the very top, in psych-type journals is difficult because a lot of my research is qualitative, not quantitative. So the only things I've got published in those more general ones are quantitative. I haven't got my qualitative stuff out there and I feel much more comfortable in qualitative than I do in quantitative, so yeah, it is more difficult.

**NICOLA So for an early career researcher [who has] never written a journal article before, what can they expect about submitting that article to a journal for review?**



WILMA First of all they have to be prepared that they might not even get to review, so that's one thing. It might come back and the editor [says], 'This is not suitable for our journal.' That would indicate that they haven't done their homework in terms of looking at the journal first. But say it gets to review, they may well get a situation like I've had one time with that very frustrating paper I had, where they might get three reviews and two reviewers have said, 'Yep this is good go ahead and publish' and the third one is being critical and the editor's come back and said, 'No, we're rejecting it'. I know that has happened to me. So you have to be prepared to see stuff [reviews] that's contradictory and it doesn't make sense. Sometimes a decision won't make sense to you, so you have to be prepared for rejection.

Don't sit and wait for that article to come back, you've got to be working on the next one and sending that to a different location. So that's what you expect, you've got to expect delays even if they say, 'Our process takes five weeks or our process takes six weeks', you can expect that it's going to be a long time. Quite often it's more than two or three months. One of the ones that I did took eight months before I got the review back and that can be frustrating because you think, 'I could be sending this somewhere else'. If it comes back rejected and you sent it out over a year ago then that can be very disheartening. That's why I ask, 'What other spin can you put on that work to send it somewhere else?' I think one of the things that we try to do is that we write too much because we try to put everything in one article rather than making sure that the length of our article is suitable as well. So, be prepared for rejection and be prepared for lengthy feedback. If it comes back and it's accepted, well, that's terrific, celebrate! If it comes back with 'Here are some [requested] changes', I think it's important to try to get to them as quickly as you can, because then you don't run into the possibility that there's a change of editorship. So no matter what else you think you've got on your plate, highly prioritise making the changes that they suggest. Getting advice from other people about the feedback that you've received [is important]. Ask them, 'Have I really addressed their feedback in doing this and so on?' Give them what they want, because at the end of the day you might sort of think, 'Oh well, I don't really agree with that' but you get it out there and so on. You can kind of rewrite it in a more convincing way with some supplementary data somewhere else and so on. So, go with the critiques.

So what else can you expect? One frustrating thing is if you get the feedback that comes back and says, 'We're rejecting it, sorry', with no feedback about how it could be improved or what you've neglected to consider. That gives you nowhere to go so you're not quite sure how you're going to redirect it and so on. Again, get advice from somebody. It can be people outside your field as I've found sometimes it's just somebody that says, 'Oh well, you know, what you've done might be interesting for this audience and here are some journals [in that area].' Be prepared for that. You might get rejected a couple of times but persistence is the key with all of this because you will crack it and once you've been published in a journal, it breaks the ice and it's easier to get published in that same journal again later on.



**NICOLA Why is that?**

WILMA Because there's the follow up kind of idea, it's possible that then people have read that article and there may be the beginning of some citation in that journal of your article, so your name kind of gets known by the reviewers. So if they've read it and they've thought it's good, they come in with a positive mindset for something that comes across their desk. Even though it's meant to be blind review, that's not necessarily a blind referee.

**NICOLA What do you think slows young academics down in their career? What things will slow you down from progressing?**

WILMA I think aiming too high, like putting all your eggs in one basket. If you aim too high and you've got that kind of delay it really slows you down. I think you can make the mistake of trying to do too many conferences, so you need to really target those because the reality is in academe, the journal article is more highly regarded than [conference papers]. You don't want too much of one thing on your CV. You don't want your CV to have like 50 conference papers and one journal article because that's not highly regarded. It's no good in terms of having 50 books and one journal article either. They do look at the spread. So I think, try out the idea on the conference but then you have to do something with it, not do the next conference paper for the next conference, you've got to really discipline yourself to take it and work on it. Be prepared for the long haul, but just keep working on it. I think people get slowed down if they are a little bit afraid to be judged by their peers. Nobody's going to look at it and say, 'Oh you know you've got terrible grammar or you've got sort of shocking spelling' or, you know, 'This makes no sense to me or it's way out there.' There are a lot of people as I found when I was starting out, that know nothing about your field. The people who gave me my best feedback on that very first article, were quantitative researchers. It was a reanalysis of historical documents and so it was completely different from what they were used to but they were willing to read it and give me some good feedback about that. I think the people who have been successful are the people who are willing to go out there and talk to people and get informal mentoring as well as the stuff that's been set up through the formal channels because sometimes, your academic supervisor might be OK and so on but they're not really interested in helping you get to the top. They sort of let you do all of the running rather than really giving you advice. So because I feel as if I got a lot of help from particular people when I started, I've always taken an interest in trying to help new people and to help them get published and so on.



So I'll give a specific example, I was talking to [a colleague] one day and she was having some frustrations around getting published. She was doing a lot of writing but [another person] was putting [their] name on first. So I just sort of talked to her, 'Well, what else have you got in your data? Because my area's in gifted, have you got anything in your data that might be about a gifted kid?' So we just chatted, she talked about this particular kid, her observations and so on. It was like, OK, we've got a good paper here because what you're talking about is peer friendships and the assumptions around peer friendships in gifted ed. So the two of us worked together on that as an article and got it published. I gave her the first authorship because it was her data even though it sort of was pretty much a 50/50 kind of deal. So I think trying to find people like that, that will work with you and get you started because then the process gets under way. So I think that holds people back, breaking the ice, knowing how to get that first one or the second one in there [published].

**NICOLA Great, I think that's a great place to end.**

# 15 Professor Sara Dolnicar

Professor Sara Dolnicar (pronounced dol-ni-char) has arguably navigated the jungle of academia very quickly and very successfully. Born in Slovenia, Sara grew up in Austria and moved to Australia in 2002. She is currently a Professor of Marketing in the School of Marketing and the Associate Dean (Research) of the Faculty of Commerce at the University of Wollongong. After receiving her PhD in 1996, Sara has been involved in extensive industrial, commercial and professional activity in both Europe and Australia. Her rapid rise to professorship is notable, as she was promoted from being an assistant professor (equivalent to lecturer/senior lecturer in Australasia) in 1994 to full professor in 2006. What might also be considered remarkable about Sara is that at the time of writing she is still in her 30s.

Since 2002, Sara has attracted almost AUD$4 million in research grants. Of note, she received the Charles G. Goeldner Article of Excellence Award from the *Journal of Travel Research* in 2004, and the Emerald Literati Highly Commended Award for Excellence in 2008. Since 1997, she has published more than 65 refereed journal articles. Sara's curriculum vitae is approximately 40-pages long which suggests an incredible commitment to her career, and it provides evidence of exceptional achievement especially in such a short period over the last 15 years.

From the mountains of Austria to the escarpment of Wollongong, Sara has successfully navigated the jungle of tourism and marketing academia to produce an outstanding international profile. She candidly shares some of the challenges she has faced, and the ethical issues she has negotiated as a supervisor, as an early career researcher and now as an established researcher and administrator.

## PROFESSIONAL DIALOGUE

**NICOLA Thank you very much Sara for being interviewed today. First of all, when and where did you receive your PhD?**

SARA In 1996 from the Vienna University of Economics and Business Administration.

**NICOLA How many publications did you get out of your PhD?**



SARA I think none, or maybe it was one, I think none. My thesis was the best thesis in the university for that year, so they published it as a monograph, but that doesn't really count in terms of publications in my discipline. In terms of journals, I might have had one journal article in a low-ranked journal. That's it, so I had one weak journal article and the monograph which was basically just a printed version of my thesis.

**NICOLA Well perhaps we can explore that more then, you got a monograph out of that but do you view it is being a real book?**

SARA No. I mean it is a real book but in my discipline that's not worth much. In my discipline what counts is journal articles published in highly ranked academic journals and from that perspective I've walked out of my PhD with nothing much really.

**NICOLA Well some of my questions are about how you went about publishing the findings of your PhD so my questions might not be pertinent.**

SARA Yes, after working in academia for a while I figured out what mattered.

**NICOLA So how did you find out about what was important?**

SARA You pick these things up when you talk to colleagues. I remember vividly going to my supervisor's office one day and asking 'Is it true that certain journals are better than others?' It was such a naive question but I really had no idea. So he listed a number of journals and I wrote them down frantically. It took me a long time to really understand the quality and positioning of journals. Only now do I feel informed about the main journals in my areas and can competently assess which kind of work I should be sending where. That's not a trivial task. I don't think that a PhD student can make that judgement. I certainly couldn't have when I was a PhD student.

**NICOLA What is a memorable experience you had as an early career academic?**

SARA I had a tremendous time as an early career academic. But I was wasting a lot of my time because I did a lot of things around the place, got involved in everything and lacked focus. But I do not regret that. Many of the skills I learned came in quite handy later. I was doing public relations for the department, I was teaching, I was doing academic and commercial research, I was writing industry reports, I was issuing a monthly research newsletter etc. I was doing all this stuff which nowadays I probably wouldn't recommend to a PhD student.



But in many ways those experiences made me who I am and I developed strengths then which I probably wouldn't have the luxury to develop anymore now. That time was very memorable to me because I enjoyed the variety of what I was doing, that stage of my career was fantastic. So I don't know that there is one single memorable experience. I can share some experiences of how I learned by making mistakes. One distinct experience I will never forget was – after I finally figured out that I needed to publish – sending a manuscript to a conference and to a journal at the same time, thinking that was very efficient. Then it dawned on me that that's probably not right. It sounds terrible when I say this now and it sounds so obviously wrong, but I think at the beginning of your career these things are just not so clear. Even today I think this line is quite blurred. Many people present papers at conferences, publish them in conference proceedings and then in journals as marginally changed versions, which I personally do not find right. Others seem to be presenting the same paper at conferences for many consecutive years. That also is questionable. Anyway, I misjudged the situation when I was starting my career. But luckily my supervisor was and is an absolutely very honourable professor (which is a reason why I'm still in academia), he heard that and politely informed me that this was not acceptable. I remember this very vividly because I thought to myself 'Oh no, what did I do?' I thought my career would end before it even got started because I made this terrible mistake. Luckily the revisions requested by the journal forced me to undertake a whole new study for the revision, so the journal paper had nothing in common with the conference paper in the end. I think those are the experiences that I remember very strongly: those where I stuffed up and learnt from it.

Working with my supervisor in itself was a memorable experience because he is such a good role model for a professor. It's very disillusioning to see the way in which many people operate in academia and that's probably also something that a book like yours might have to touch upon: exploitation of young people, piggybacking students' publications. A lot of dishonest and dishonourable things are happening. I was in the absolutely luxurious position that I was never exploited. Well, subsequently a few people tried. But when I was in training, when I was most vulnerable and the perfect victim for exploitation (because I had no clue what the whole game is about) I never was exploited, instead I was taught the merits of collaboration within and across disciplinary boundaries. I was lucky enough to work with people who took good care of me. For instance, my supervisor insisted that everything we ever published listed authors in alphabetical order. His last name started with M, so he was always listed after me. This kind of behaviour gave me the impression that academia is a very honourable trade and made it attractive to me.

I see nowadays people are still struggling massively with issues of co-authorship and author order. When we have our introductory sessions for HDR [higher degree by research] students, I always say that if they are going to publish with their supervisor, they need to clarify the rules of the collaboration. Of course this is not an easy conversation to have, but it is much easier to have it than regret not having had it when it is too late.

**NICOLA What are the things that slow you down as an academic, what can you get caught up in that distracts you from success?**

SARA That's interesting. Now that you made me talk about all of these good old times I might have changed my point of view. Half an hour ago I would have said, 'Nowadays you really can't afford any distractions. You have to be focused, you basically have to start publishing before you've got your PhD because if you ever want a research career you will need those publications on your CV [curriculum vitae]. If you want a postdoctorate fellowship after your PhD you've got to have a pretty strong track record to even have a chance.' On the other hand, after having chatted with you now, it's a real shame that that's how it appears to be nowadays. Because that's the time where you learn and it's a real shame that it's almost not possible anymore to 'waste' a bit of your time broadening your horizon by organising a conference etc. Such activities do not help much on the CV, but they actually mean a lot in terms of the experience that you have and the contacts you make. So, what distracts you? Teaching distracts you, all kinds of governance tasks distract you, but I think it's not fair to say that early career academics should not be doing any of that. My students, I want them involved in a little bit of everything but I'm quite strict with respect to the amount of time they dedicate to such activities. It makes no sense to me that students on full scholarships teach eight hours a week. I think it's an ill-advised student who does that. So, I guess, people need to know what they want. Some people want to do the PhD and want to be teachers. Well if that's the case then that's fine but people who are doing a PhD and want to make sure they have a strong research career must somehow cope with the challenge to still make a variety of experiences but do it in small amounts. So, for instance, because I know that my students need jobs, I want them to have teaching on their CVs. But what I tell them is, do [teach only] one tutorial. It sounds terrible because of course the first tutorial is the most work. If you do five, four of them are cheap repeats. But in terms of the total time they have, one tute [tutorial, usually a one-hour session per week with 24 students] gives them exposure and experience. One tute gives them something on their CV, but it actually keeps the amount of time commitment low enough that they can still focus on their research.



**NICOLA So what would you say, if somebody else wanted to progress successfully like you have so quickly, what would you advise them to do?**

SARA I think there is just no magic to it. I think the honest truth is that I cannot sit still. I can't sit still. If I'm at home I've got to do something, I've got to improve the garage, I've got to clean something. That's inbuilt, hardwired. I think some people have to fight to get themselves to do something. I have to fight to just hang out and relax. I genuinely enjoy the stuff I'm doing and whether it's research or whether it's fixing the garage, it doesn't matter. I enjoy working. I think some people expect tips of how to 'play it smart'. I do not have any. I think if you are genuinely interested in what you are doing, you will do well. If you are not genuinely interested, it's just not going to work. If you don't like research you're never going to be able to force yourself to do good research.

But the decision is quite simple, you do it or you don't do it. If you're not enjoying it, well find yourself something else you're going to enjoy. Maybe a common mistake people make is that they're not true to themselves at the very beginning. They do not find themselves a topic they're really passionate about. And that's a very bad starting point.

When I first came here I came as a senior lecturer, I had massive problems, cultural problems. Nobody here liked me much. Quite the opposite: people thought I was too loud, too opinionated, too confrontational. Admittedly at that time I was not so fond of Australians either. Anyway, I found myself in this situation where I was alone in a country very, very far away from home and my social support network. Clearly people here disliked me and did not understand how I operated and I didn't understand how they operated. In that situation, work performance became very much an issue of survival or, if you want, personal pride. I really only had two options in that situation: I could either go back home and say I'm a total loser and admit that Australia beat me. Or I could say, 'Well if I'm going, I'm going on my terms.' And I guess that's what I decided. If I was going to leave this country I was not going to leave it as a loser. Although this was not a pleasant situation or feeling, it certainly motivated me to work harder and to perform.

So I quickly realised that everyone in Australia, which is quite different from Austria, talks about ARC [Australian Research Council] grants. In Austria, we have a grant system but it's a lot less important, so in Austria it's still top journal publications that primarily matter. Competitive grants are just not as important as they are in Australia. So everyone kept talking about ARC grants and I came to the conclusion that if I wanted to be taken seriously I had to have one of those. I just spent all my time in the Research Office with the then grants manager learning how to write a good grant application. And then the first one was knocked back, and the second one got knocked back. But eventually I got one. It felt great, like a real achievement.

So maybe this was my strongest driver during my first years in Australia: survival. It sounds very fundamental but I think it is true that in academia your life insurance is your CV.

**NICOLA Have you an anecdote you can share about a frustrating experience about publishing in a journal?**

SARA Oh god, where shall I start, there's so many. I had so many frustrating experiences, nothing to tell a good story about. When you first get a frustrating one you think it's a terrible disaster but over time it's the standard, so I just don't think that they're so frustrating anymore. In fact, to be quite honest, as a general rule I prefer if they reject me than if they give me a half-hearted revise/resubmit.

**NICOLA What about your reactions to rejections?**

SARA Oh well, I get totally annoyed, of course. Actually, less so nowadays. It's just part of the job. But I used to get very upset. I remember my colleague Fritz. He is a little bit older and a little bit wiser than I am. So when we first started publishing together we got revise/resubmits and I would just smash the reviewers in the letter where you get to respond to the reviewers. Fritz's most challenging job of collaborating with me was to censor my text. That has changed a lot over time. In many ways I was more idealistic then, but also more suicidal with respect to publishing. Now I understand the process much better. Years ago when someone criticised me I thought, 'No, that person's wrong and I've got to explain to that person that they're wrong.' Now I think, 'Oh well, just another frustrated reviewer who's had a bad day and needs to polish up their ego.' So best to tell them, 'You're the best and I'm so happy you found that typo and, yes, I fixed the typo.'

Another anecdote I can tell you relates to my sustainable tourism project. I wrote two manuscripts on different aspects of an empirical study I conducted and submitted them to two journals. Reviewers always need to criticise something. Very few reviewers I think have the self-esteem to write 'this is actually a really nice paper let's publish it', so they are always going [to] have to pick on something. So the funny thing in that situation was that the reviewers had picked on exactly different aspects, so literally I was able to swap the papers, send it to the reverse journal with some additional changes and both journals were delighted to see that I have followed their very major requests for revision. We just could not believe it. What are the chances of that happening?



I believe that researchers need to be idealistic but then on the other hand the way the industry works makes it actually very hard to be idealistic because you have to permanently think about the politics involved. For example, my supervisor was the first to introduce a certain methodology into tourism and research. One day I read a recent issue of one of the A-star journals in tourism where the author claimed to be introducing that very same methodology to tourism and did not even quote my supervisor. I was really angry and felt that this was not right. It was not right that this article was published. Either the author had not done his homework or the reviewers had not. Driven by idealism (and naivety) I sent a very firm email to both the editor and the author of this article saying that it was wrong not to cite my supervisor, that it was in fact misleading not to do so. I never received a response. And for many years I regretted sending this email because it meant that one of the three A-star journals was probably not going to be keenly awaiting to publish my manuscripts. Now, many years later, everyone has forgotten, I am publishing in and reviewing for that journal and I am proud of sending those emails. I think it was right to do so, but as an early career researcher you just don't have the market power yet to do that and not worry about possible negative consequences.

**NICOLA What would you have to say about nepotism and gatekeeping in academia?**

SARA What do you mean by gatekeeping?

**NICOLA Well, how that there are people who will check to see whether you fit in with their plan or their ideas of the world before they let you through.**

SARA That fits into what I call exploitation in the widest sense. I think nepotism is more of an issue of academic management than it is one of academic publishing. Yes, I think that there is what you could call nepotism amongst journals but I actually don't know that it's intended as such. Let's put it this way: if I'm an editor of a journal, and if I get a manuscript from someone who I know has written 50 good articles or I get the same manuscript from someone I've never heard of, it could be construed as nepotism that the person who's written 50 good articles is going to have by far a better chance of getting published. But if you look at it from the editor's perspective, nepotism is probably not the driving force. It is more the confidence that you've built in someone's research abilities over many years. And it may even be that a journal is keen to publish work from an author who is internationally acknowledged. I don't think that in publishing it is as bad, and I'm saying this not as a beneficiary of this game. In the case of marketing journals, for instance, there does seem to be a distinct North American bias, so I'm at the losing end. But still I think that editors are actually not publishing their mate's work, they publish work they genuinely think is the best work.

In any organisation, however, there is nepotism. During my first years in academia I was lucky to encounter no nepotism, very little politics and very little game playing. That's what I chose to sign up for when I became an academic. Subsequently, I noticed it's not like that everywhere. Other extremes are supervisors putting their names on students' publications without having contributed a sentence, or supervisors preventing people from submitting their PhD until they do enough 'slavery work' for them. I have seen it happen on all continents, it's not an Australian thing. It is very sad if people start off in such an environment and I have little advice for them. How do you get out of it? You probably just need to change the environment. If I had had a supervisor that would have operated like that I would have done my PhD and gone out of academia because I think that's totally unacceptable and in the end I must say people need to stand up for themselves but that means conflict. Australians in particular are not good at conflict. For me, rather than nepotism and gatekeeping, I think it's more an issue of exploitation at the early stages of people's careers. I think what early career researchers need to do is to resist the temptation to be opportunistic and that's very hard. They need to say what they want to do; they need to choose a topic they will be passionate about and do high-quality work, without cutting corners. Otherwise they become players from day one and then they can hardly complain if they end up finding themselves in the middle of politics throughout their careers.

**NICOLA OK, what would you like to say about your observations about the process of getting published within journals, especially in prestigious ones?**

SARA Well, I must be honest. I think that on the whole it's a pretty fair process, that doesn't mean that we always get what we want. I've seen the other side now. I've been on editorial boards, I've been a reviewer, and I have to say quite frankly there's a lot of weak work being submitted. I am convinced that if someone writes a good manuscript it will get published. I have absolutely no doubt they're going to get it published. I'm not saying you will get it published in the first journal you're going to submit it to but if it's a good manuscript you will get it published and you will get it published in a solid journal. Some advice I got from a professor in Vienna was to always submit to the best journals. If you submit to a bad journal, you're going to get bad reviewers, you're going to get useless feedback. I'm not saying everyone should be submitting to A-star journals, but the better the journal the better the editorial board and the reviewers. The better the feedback you're going to get, the higher the chances you're going to get a few rejections but the only way you're going to learn is to get rejections, so you will figure out eventually what works and what does not work.



I remember my first rejection. It was my first conference submission. I basically slapped a few PowerPoint slides together and put it into a paper, it was totally unacceptable, it was not a paper, but nobody told me and I just had a go at it. So I submitted this and they said that it made little contribution and for weeks I was upset and angry because it was original, because it was in the early stages of neural networks being used in marketing. So the feedback that it was not original was really wrong but my paper should have never been accepted anyway. But I didn't understand that at that point. Had I given it to people around me they would have told me that it's not suitable for publication. So I think that the peer review system generally works. The better the journal the more rigorous the review system is going to be, which means the success rate is lower but it also means that your learning opportunity is a lot higher.

But there is always an aspect of luck in every submission as well. Luck with the reviewer selection etc. So it is absolutely OK to view a submission as buying a lottery ticket, but with academia being highly competitive, it has to be a very good manuscript. A bad manuscript is not a lottery ticket, it never makes it past the editor's desk. Sometimes I get manuscripts where people still have sections marked with Xs because clearly they got fed up at some point and submitted it and haven't proofread it and haven't actually included the citations. I do not even look at such manuscripts. When you submit a manuscript you have to ask yourself: is this the best, best, best possible work I can do? When I write papers or grants applications, the first version and the one I submit have absolutely nothing in common anymore. So, yes, there are weirdos involved in the journal review process and, yes, there are frustrated reviewers who have a bad family life and therefore nag you – that's all true but I still think that if you have a strong manuscript it will get published.



Another thing I think people don't realise is that whatever is out there under your name is there for eternity. You cannot afford to risk your reputation for a quick publication. If you publish bad work or continuously publish in bad journals, this works against you. So it's very hard nowadays for early career researchers. They are under tremendous pressure to produce research outputs and the temptation to take short cuts is huge.

The other thing I've noticed more recently is a trend of outsourcing aspects of the research work, substantial aspects of the research work. For example, outsourcing the literature review. I can live with that. But then they start outsourcing the data collection, which I have more trouble with. Then they start outsourcing the data analysis. This to me is highly problematic. I have even heard someone say that they should really pay someone to write it up because, after all, they are not an expert writer. I think early career researchers are really harming themselves by taking such an approach. If substantial bits of the research have been outsourced like that, quality control becomes a major issue. If I give someone else my data to analyse, how do I know they've done it right, but it's my name that's on top of the manuscript! Maybe it does require more inner strength in terms of sticking to your principles nowadays than it did years ago when you just had freedom like I did to potter around a few years to try to find out what this job's all about and what you want to do. Now they're thrown right into the deep water and expected to swim and the temptation is very high to not learn the trade but learn the tricks of the trade straight away.

**NICOLA Looking back over your career is there anything that you would do differently if you had the chance again?**

SARA Oh absolutely, I think that I also took short cuts, but I took short cuts that I didn't know about. So, for instance, for the kind of research I'm doing, I should have done a statistics degree, but I didn't know that then. And I never did, well why, because I was not naturally interested in stats, so I did a psychology degree and I did a business degree. I did a psychology degree because that's what I was passionate about. I did a business degree because I said I'm going to have to earn money, who knows if psychologists are going to be hired. So, now I lack those statistics skills and that's really sad because at this stage of my career I simply do not have the time anymore to learn an entire new discipline from scratch, so I'm really dependent on my collaborators. Luckily I work with statisticians that are outstanding and that I get along with and we work well together but the truth is I'd rather have the confidence myself. So, I have made short cuts myself which are preventing me from making it a lot further than I ever will make it.

**NICOLA Finally, is there anything, any other advice you'd give to early career researchers?**



SARA Primarily they need to be honest to themselves in that they need to ask the question, 'Why am I doing this?' If they're doing this because they have some illusion that academia is a cosy job that will make it easy to focus on the kids and the family, I think that's a very bad start and I don't think they're going to be happy in this career. I think they really need to honestly answer the question, 'Is that what I am passionate about?' If not, they will struggle their whole career.

I would really encourage them to collaborate. I think that collaboration in the sciences is a necessity so scientists are very good at it. But in the social sciences we think we can lock ourselves in our room and just quietly work alone. My feeling from my career is that the most exciting things I've done and also the most original research that I have produced was with people who know something I don't know. The best papers that I've written are with my stats colleagues because I come up with a problem and I think aloud about the problem, they're fascinated by the problem, they start thinking aloud about the methods and suddenly we come up with something that's a new method that solves a really relevant problem and those are things you never, ever, ever achieve alone. I wish people would see the intrinsic benefits of collaboration.

Another thing, people are very protective about their intellectual property. People tend to think, 'Oh, I've invented something, well I better hang on to it and sleep on it so nobody sees it! I'm not going to put it online because someone could steal it.' That is a totally wrong instinct people have. The best way to protect your intellectual property is to get it out there and make sure that people know it's your intellectual property. I think this tendency prevents a lot of people from cooperation and that is really, really sad. I try to collaborate with anyone who wants to collaborate. Sometimes it works, sometimes it does not and sometimes you are really lucky and you develop a life-long collaboration with another researcher that is rewarding and productive. For early career researchers it's similar: if you want to collaborate with people you will probably have to do a lot of the foot work. But that's your entry point and if you find valuable research partners you develop a continuing collaboration. For example, my best ever research assistant, Katrina. She has been working with me for four or five years now. She is currently doing her honours degree. Katrina for me is actually the perfect early career researcher. In her particular case she's actually chosen to go into industry so she won't do a PhD, at least not now, maybe she will come back and do it later, but over those last few years she has done so much work for me, a lot of [it] is not particularly stimulating, like formatting papers according to journal guidelines, recoding data sets, I don't even remember, like everything, everything, everything and she did it without ever complaining. Of course, that's a bit different because she's an RA [research assistant] and she's paid to do this kind of work. But it has certainly paid off for her. Over the years she got more and more responsible tasks to work on and now she has two A-star publications, one A and one B publication on her CV. She would have not had this output if she hadn't started from scratch and she's probably the person who I would give anything at anytime and trust that she would do it right because she learnt it from scratch. If people want to learn they've got to be willing to just bite the bullet sometimes and say, yep, fine, no problem I'll do the questionnaire, no problem I'll enter the data. If you are too vain for this, if you're already too good for all of this at the early career stages, well where are you going to go?



Talk with people from other disciplines, that's another one. Everyone talks about interdisciplinary research but very few people are actually courageous enough to genuinely jump into it because it takes a lot of time to initially learn about other people's disciplines. I mean when I started working with my colleagues from statistics, we were sitting in a room and I did not understand half the words they used and they did not understand half the words I used. It probably took us two years before we had the first paper out.

What else? Work with students, supervise students. People think students are a key performance indicator on its own. If you can find a motivated, smart student, they become a team member and both you and the student will benefit from the joint work. Again I have one example: my first ever PhD student, Melanie. Someone sent her to me because she wanted to do a PhD. So this lady, highly pregnant, 'rolls' into my office and says, 'I want to do a

PhD.' I said, 'I am new in this country. I have nothing to offer you. Actually, I am under pressure to get one of those ARC grants. So if you are serious and if you want a scholarship and if you're interested to work with me on one of those applications, we can do this together.' Melanie took the risk and did. We jointly wrote a grant application about public schools and how they could improve their image. We didn't get that grant. But I got a different one and I was able to give her the scholarship. At that time I did not have a cent in research funding to pay her for her contribution to the grant application. She was working for hours and hours for absolutely nothing but a small chance of getting a scholarship out of it. Look from her perspective – this is how it must have looked: here's this lunatic lady who nobody likes and who's basically saying, 'I have no guarantees for you but if you want you can work for me for free for awhile.' Anyway, she just took her chances, got her scholarship, completed her PhD and now she's got a five-year research-only postdoctorate position (and four children). That's a good example of what you can achieve when you are motivated, hard-working and willing to take a risk.



**NICOLA Great, and I think that's a great place to end.**[1]

1 Please note: Katrina and Melanie both gave their permission for their names to be included in this interview.

# Conclusion: Negotiating the Crowded Jungle – Acknowledge Successful Navigation

Professors are human and have worked long and hard for their success. The latter aspects are the predominant factor for their achievement. Placing professors on a pedestal in praise of their success seems natural, but their trajectories towards success are not a guarded secret. What is evident is that professors are normal, intelligent people who work hard, and who have got their work published in journals that have a similar and sympathetic bent to them. They have the ability to write, think and search for appropriate places to publish their work. We all have that same ability. Usually, they have also had longevity, of which not all people are blessed.

## BUILDING A CASTLE IN THE JUNGLE

Why would anyone build a castle in a jungle? The fact remains that many academics are only about themselves and their work. They seek to rise above everyone else by self-promotion and by only talking about what interests them or is important to them. For them, 'It's all about me'. Their self-importance means they have no hesitation in 'borrowing' ideas, or plagiarizing them, or using study leave applications from other less-ranked academics as their own. Their concern is building their own castle where they can look down on everyone else. From the top of their castle, they can be supported by other lesser-known academics and postgraduate students who can help prop up their walls and make them look impressive. Fortunately, there are not many of these academics in the jungle. But, you will eventually realise that these 'castle' academics are not interested in you or your work or your career; they are interested in how you can help build their castle.

Other academics are arrogant, simply because they have an inflated view of their ability and their (assisted) success. It is in their best interests to question you, to try you, to challenge you, to disagree with you, because in doing so they are validating the space and position they currently occupy. If they agreed with all your new ideas, they would in fact be destabilising the foundation on which they have established themselves. What would their experience count for then?

The ones who are secure in their skin are not apprehensive about change and innovation. They are not scared of affirming talent, initiative and foresight. Those who lack these things will not be remembered as you go about attaining your professorship. Therefore, creativity, drive, focus and tenacity will be rewarded in the long run despite those persons who pull you down in order to lift themselves up. Such is the nature of primary/elementary school playground behaviour.

Can you think critically and express yourself clearly? Then that is the first step to carving out and establishing your academic career. This is my own pep talk at the age of 33 where I often feel overwhelmed at the immensity and depth and extent of what I need to do in order to establish myself. More often than not I receive discouragement rather than encouragement and this has left me feeling despondent in many forms. While being in a supportive faculty environment does indeed help, no one else is going to write that paper or article for you. You are responsible for ensuring your success, and this book has hopefully helped you to realise what is needed to publish journal articles from your PhD, one of the many steps in successful navigation of the academic jungle. You must be able to clearly write your ideas in a logical manner. Any form of writing needs to have a purpose, but probably more important than that is the fact that other people need to be able to read it and know what you are saying and why. Black et al. illuminated this aptly: 'Many papers are rejected simply because the editor and review board can't figure out what they're supposed to be saying' (1998: 88).

Once you have an idea for an article, the best thing to do is to think about what it will look like, then find the appropriate forum for its presentation, then finish writing it. Do not do what I did, and write four articles from your thesis, and then submit them to journals that you think would be OK. I had the right idea in that I created themes, but I needed to get an idea of what each article was about, and then craft that article to meet the aims, scope, readership and word length for each of the particular journals in which I was interested. Impact factor and journal ranking does not matter if you have good research.

Every time I write something and it is about 90 per cent done, I have a meltdown where I think it is not good enough, that I am a fraud, that people will think I am daft and that there is no way I am going to meet the deadline. But then I do. I finish procrastinating. I get into the zone. I meet the deadline and I produce something of which I am proud. Keep that in mind. You can do it too.

In a rare glimpse of candour from Professor Duncan Watts, an eminent mathematician who is famous for his work on networks and the small world phenomenon, he highlights how the work that is published in journals is a result of many years of work, many rewrites and edits, and a hefty commitment to excellence and scholarly endeavour.

> *The science of textbooks is typically a dry and intimidating affair. Unfolding in a relentless march of logic from apparently impossible questions to seemingly indisputable conclusions, textbook science is hard enough to follow, let alone emulate. And even when science is presented as an act of discovery, an achievement of humans, the process by which they actually figured it out remains cloaked in mystery. My dominant memory from years of physics and math courses is the depressing sense that no normal person could actually do this stuff.*
>
> *But real science doesn't work that way. As I eventually learned, real science occurs in the same messy ambiguous world that scientists struggle to clarify, and is done by real people who suffer the same kind of limitations and confusions as anybody else. The characters in this story are, one and all, talented people who have worked hard throughout their lives to succeed as scientists. But they are also entirely human. I know that because I know them, and I know that we have struggled and often failed together, only to pick ourselves up to try again. Our papers get rejected, our ideas don't work out, we misunderstand things that later seem obvious, and most of the time we feel frustrated or just plain stupid. But we struggle on, the journey being every bit as much the point as the destination. Doing science is really a lot like doing anything else, but by the time it gets out into the larger world and everyone reads about it in books, it has been so reworked and refined that it takes on an aura of inevitability it never hard in the making. (Watts 2003: 14–15)*

What Watts makes clear is that scholarly endeavours and accomplishments are undertaken and completed by normal human beings. We should not feel intimidated by these great achievements and contributions; we should be inspired.

We should also keep in mind that while those that review for journals are gatekeepers in the sense that they will not allow 'rubbish' to be published, they are there to perform a function. Reviewers are there to exhort you to enhance and craft your work into cohesive, relevant and precise articles. Those that take on the important and pro-bono work of reviewing, have also taken on the mantle of promoting scholarly knowledge.

This book was not originally intended to be a self-help or advice book. It showcases others' experiences, and my experience in a bid to illuminate the density of the jungle, and how you might navigate it for your own journey. As others have said, you must believe in yourself, because if you do not no one else will either. In one way, it was a cathartic process for me. In being able to put my journey into words, I have been able to reflect upon the process with more rationalism. I am happy that I am able to contribute to others' journeys, encourage them in their trajectories towards their desired destination, and help you to negotiate this crowded jungle.



In order to survive and successfully navigate the jungle, you need to have plenty of supplies and stamina. You need to keep your bearings and spend ample time thinking about how you fit in to the jungle, which paths are right for you to take and whether more difficult paths are worth the effort. As it is your own solo journey making and marking your way through the dense foliage, only you can figure out how to deal with your particular challenges. But I encourage you to seek out other travellers who you can assist and be assisted by as you seek to reach your destination(s).

# References


Aitchison, C., Kamler, B. and Lee, A. (eds) (2010), *Publishing Pedagogies for the Doctorate and Beyond* (London: Routledge).

AJET (Australasian Journal of Educational Technology) (2008), 'Editorial 24(3)' [online], <http://www.ascilite.org.au/ajet/ajet24/editorial24-3.html>, accessed 10 February 2009.

ARC (Australian Research Council) (2009a), Australian and New Zealand Standard Research Classification (ANZSRC) [webpage], <http://www.arc.gov.au/era/ANZSRC.htm>, accessed 13 January 2010.

—— (2009b), ERA 2010: Ranked outlets [webpage], <http://www.arc.gov.au/era/era_journal_list.htm>, accessed 13 January 2010.

—— (2009c), Tiers for the Australian Ranking of Journals [webpage], <http://www.arc.gov.au/era/tiers_ranking.htm>, accessed 13 January 2010.

Atkinson, R. and McLoughlin, C. (2008), 'Editorial 24(1): The Decision to Retire AJET's Printed Version', *Australasian Journal of Educational Technology* 24:1, iii–viii.

Black, D., Brown, S., Day, A. and Race, P. (1998), *500 Tips for Getting Published: A Guide for Educators, Researchers and Professionals* (London: Kogan Page).

Boden, R., Epstein, D. and Kenway, D. (2005), *Building Your Academic Career.* Volume 1, Academics' Support Kit (London: Sage).

Boden, R., Kenway, J. and Epstein, D. (2005), *Getting Started on Research.* Volume 2, Academics' Support Kit (London: Sage).

Booth, P. (2008), 'Rereading Fandom: MySpace Character Personas and Narrative Identification', *Critical Studies in Media Communication* 25:5, 514–36.

Bourdieu, P., Chamboredon, J.-C. and Passeron, J.-C. (trans Nice, R.) (1991), *The Craft of Sociology: Epistemological Preliminaries* (Berlin: Walter de Gruyter & Co).

Brabazon, T. (ed.) (2008), *The Revolution Will Not Be Downloaded: Dissent in the Digital Age* (Farnham, Surrey: Ashgate).

—— (2009a), 'YouTube has merit, but enough already of cat videos', *The Times Higher Education*, 2 December 2009 [webpage], <http://www.timeshighereducation.co.uk/story.asp?sectioncode=26&storycode=409416&c=1>, accessed 18 January 2010.

—— (2009b), 'Forget the Spanx, leaders of tomorrow', *The Times Higher Education*, 9 September 2009 [webpage], <http://www.timeshighereducation.co.uk/story.asp?sectioncode=26&storycode=408077>, accessed 13 January 2010.

Calhoun, C., LiPuma, E. and Postone, M. (eds) (1993), *Bourdieu: Critical Perspectives* (Cambridge: Polity Press).

Cantor, J.A. (1993), *A Guide to Academic Writing* (Westport, CT: Greenwood Press).

Carolan, B.V. (2008), 'The Structure of Educational Research: The Role of Multivocality in Promoting Cohesion in an Article Interlock Network', *Social Networks* 30:1, 69–82.

Cham, J. (2008), 'Your (real) impact factor', PHD comics. Available: <http://www.phdcomics.com/comics/archive.php?comicid=1108>, accessed 14 January 2010.



Common Ground (2008), 'Book08' [webpage], http://booksandpublishing.com/conference-2010/ accessed 26 January 2010.

—— (2010), 'The Common Ground Journal Publishing Model' [webpage], <http://www.cgpublisher.com/publishers/30/web/publishing_policy.html#JPM>, accessed 16 January 2010.

Connell, R.W. (1995), *Masculinities* (Crows Nest, NSW: Allen & Unwin).

Craswell, G. (2005), *Writing for Academic Success: A Postgraduate Guide* (London: Sage).

Day, A. (1996), *How to get Research Published in Journals* (Aldershot, Hants: Gower).

—— (2008), *How to get Research Published in Journals*, 2nd Edition (Farnham, Surrey: Gower).

Deleuze, G. and Guattari, F. (trans. Massumi, B.) (1987), *A Thousand Plateaus* (Minneapolis: University of Minnesota Press).

Epstein, D., Boden, R. and Kenway, J. (2005), *Teaching and Supervision.* Volume 4 (London: Sage).

Epstein, D., Kenway, J. and Boden, R. (2005), *Writing for Publication.* Volume 3 (London: Sage).

Evans, J., Davies, J. and Wright, J. (eds) (2004), *Body Knowledge and Control: Studies in the Sociology of Physical Education and Health* (London: Routledge).

Gale, T. (1998), Methodological 'maps' and key assumptions: A framework for understanding research. Paper presented at the Postgraduate Research Weekend, Graduate School of Education, Faculty of Education and Creative Arts, Central Queensland University, 16–17 May 1998.

Gard, M. and Wright, J. (2005), *The Obesity Epidemic: Science, Morality and Ideology* (London: Routledge).

Hall, G. (2008), *Digitize This Book! The Politics of New Media, or Why We Need Open Access Now* (Minneapolis: University of Minnesota Press).

Harding, S. (1986), *The Science Question in Feminism* (New York: Cornell University Press).

—— (1991), *Whose Science? Whose Knowledge? Thinking from Women's Lives* (New York: Cornell University Press).

Harman, E., McMenemy, S., Montagnes, I. and Bucci, C. (eds) (2003), *The Thesis and the Book: A Guide for First-Time Academic Authors*, 2nd Edition (Toronto, ON: University of Toronto Press).

HEFCE (Higher Education Funding Council for England) (2009), rae 2008: Research Assessment Exercise [webpage], <http://www.rae.ac.uk/>, accessed 13 January 2010.

Herrington, A. and Herrington, J. (2006a), *Effective Use of the Internet: Keeping Professionals Working in Rural Australia* (Barton, ACT: RIRDC).

—— (2006b), *Authentic Learning Environments in Higher Education* (Hershey, PA: Information Science Publishing).



Herrington, J., Herrington, A., Mantei, J., Olney, I. and Ferry, B. (eds) (2009), *New Technologies, New Pedagogies: Mobile Learning in Higher Education*, Faculty of Education, University of Wollongong. Available: <http://ro.uow.edu.au/newtech/>, accessed 15 January 2010.

Herrington, J., Reeves, T.C. and Oliver, R. (2010), *A Guide to Authentic e-learning* (London: Routledge).

Hesse-Biber, S.N. and Leckenby, D. (2004), 'How feminists practice social research', in Hesse-Biber and Yaiser (eds).

Hesse-Biber, S.N. and Yaiser, M. L. (eds) (2004), *Feminist Perspectives on Social Research* (New York: Oxford University Press).

Hickey-Moody, A.C. (2008), 'Performing New Spaces: The Theatre of Urban', *Critical Studies in Education* 49:2, 199–203.

Hookway, N. (2008), '"Entering the Blogosphere": Some Strategies for using Blogs in Social Research', *Qualitative Research* 8:1, 91–113.

Huff, A.S. (1999), *Writing for Scholarly Publication* (London: Sage).

in-cites (2008), Journals ranked by impact [webpage], <http://www.incites.com/research/2006/may_22_2006-1.html>, accessed 15 January 2010.

Johnson, N.F (2007), *Teenage Technological Experts: Bourdieu and the Performance of Expertise*, Unpublished Doctoral Thesis (Geelong, VIC: Deakin University).

—— (2007), 'Framing the Integration of Computers in Beginning Teacher Professional Development', *Computers in New Zealand Schools*, 19:3, 25–32, 44. Available: <http://ro.uow.edu.au/edupapers/26>, accessed 15 January 2010.

—— (2009a), *The Multiplicities of Internet Addiction: The Misrecognition of Leisure and Learning* (Farnham, Surrey: Ashgate).

—— (2009b), 'Cyber-relations in the Field of Home Computer use for Leisure: Bourdieu and Teenage Technological Experts', *E-Learning* 6:2, 187–97. Available: http://www.wwwords.co.uk/elea/content/pdfs/6/issue6_2.asp#4, accessed 15 January 2010.

—— (2009c), 'Teenage Technological Experts' Views of Schooling', *Australian Educational Researcher* 36:1, 59–72. Available: http://www.aare.edu.au/aer/contents.htm#v36_1, accessed 15 January 2010.

—— (2009d), 'Generational Differences in Beliefs about Technological Expertise', *New Zealand Journal of Educational Studies* 44:1, 31–46.

—— (2009e), 'Exchanging Online Narratives for Leisure: A Legitimate Learning Space', *International Journal of Emerging Technologies and Society* 7:1, 15–27. Available: http://www.swinburne.edu.au/hosting/ijets/journal/V7N1/vol7num1-article2.html, accessed 15 January 2010.

—— (2009f), 'Contesting Binaries: Teenage Girls as Technological Experts', *Gender, Technology and Development* 13:3, 365–383.



Johnson, N.F., Macdonald, D.C. and Brabazon, T. (2008), 'Rage Against the Machine? Symbolic Violence in E-Learning Supported Tertiary Education', *E-Learning* 5:3, 275–83. Available: <http://www.wwwords.co.uk/elea/content/pdfs/5/issue5_3.asp>, accessed 15 January 2010.

Johnson, N.F., Rowan, L. and Lynch, J. (2006), 'Constructions of Gender in Computer Magazine Advertisements: Confronting the Literature', *Studies in Media and Information Literacy Education,* 6:1. Available: http://ro.uow.edu.au/edupapers/19, accessed 15 January 2010.

Kamler, B. (2010), 'Revise and Resubmit: The Role of Publication Brokers', in Aitchison et al. (eds).

Kenway, J., Boden, R. and Epstein, D. (2005), *Winning and Managing Research Funding*. Volume 5 (London: Sage).

Kenway, J., Epstein, D. and Boden, R. (2005), *Building Networks*. Volume 6 (London: Sage).

Kenway, J., Gough, N. and Hughes, M. (1998), *Publishing in Refereed Academic Journals: A Pocket Guide* (Geelong, VIC: Deakin Centre for Education and Change).

Lamp, J. (2010), ERA Journal Rankings Access [website], <http://lamp.infosys.deakin.edu.au/era/>, accessed 13 January 2010. The final lists of rankings as well as the previous draft lists are available at the same website.

LiPuma, E. (1993), 'Culture and the Concept of Culture in a Theory of Practice', in Calhoun et al. (eds).

Lloyd, G. (1993), *The Male of Reason: 'Male' and 'Female' in Western Philosophy* (London: Routledge).

Lockyer, L., Bennett, S., Agostinho, S. and Harper, B. (eds) (2008), *Handbook of Research on Learning Design and Learning Objects: Issues, Applications, and Technologies* (2 Volumes) (Hershey, PA: Information Science Reference).

Luey, B. (2002), *Handbook for Academic Authors*, 4th Edition (Cambridge: Cambridge University Press).

Morritt, H. (1997), *Women and Computer Based Technologies: A Feminist Perspective*, (Lanham, MD: University Press of America).

Schaef, A.W. (1987), *When Society Becomes an Addict* (San Francisco: Harper & Row).

Science Gateway (2009), Journal impact factors [webpage], <http://www.sciencegateway.org/impact/>, accessed 13 January 2010.

—— (2010), High impact journals [webpage], <http://www.sciencegateway.org/rank/index.html>, accessed 15 January 2010.

Spender, D. (1995), *Nattering on the Net: Women, Power and Cyberspace* (North Melbourne: Spinifex).

Springer (2010), Languages and Literature [webpage], <http://www.springer.com/linguistics/languages+&+literature/journal/10583>, accessed 15 January 2010.

Surowiecki, J. (2004), *The Wisdom of Crowds: Why the Many Are Smarter Than the Few and How Collective Wisdom Shapes Business, Economies, Societies and Nations* (New York, NY: Double Day).





University of Wollongong Research Online <http://ro.uow.edu.au>, (date accessed 15/1/2010). (Research Online is an open access digital archive promoting the scholarly output of the University of Wollongong, Australia.)

Vialle, W. and Perry, J. (1995), *Nurturing Multiple Intelligences in the Australian Classroom* (Cheltenham, VIC: Hawker Brownlow Education).

—— (2002), *Teaching through the Eight Intelligences* (Cheltenham, VIC: Hawker Brownlow Education).

Vialle, W. and Rogers, K.B. (2009), *Educating the Gifted Learner* (Terrigal, NSW: David Barlow Publishing).

Wager, E., Godlee, F. and Jefferson, T. (2002), *How to Survive Peer Review* (London: BMJ Books).

Watts, D.J. (2003), *Six Degrees: The Science of a Connected Age* (New York: W.W. Norton & Company).

Webb, J., Schirato, T. & Danaher, G. (2002), *Understanding Bourdieu* (Crows Nest, NSW: Allen & Unwin).

Wright, J. and Harwood, V. (eds) (2009), *The Bio-politics of the 'Obesity Epidemic': Governing Bodies* (London: Routledge).

Wright, J., MacDonald, D. and Burrows, L. (eds) (2004), *Critical Inquiry and Problem-solving in Physical Education* (London: Routledge).

# Index

For Product Safety Concerns and Information please contact our EU representative GPSR@taylorandfrancis.com Taylor & Francis Verlag GmbH, Kaufingerstraße 24, 80331 München, Germany